BASKETRY TODAY
WITH MATERIALS FROM NATURE

BASKETRY TODAY
WITH MATERIALS FROM NATURE

Weaving · Twining   Pine Needles · Plaiting · Coiling · Free Form

DONA Z. MEILACH • DEE MENAGH

Crown Publishers, Inc.   New York

© 1979 by Dona Z. Meilach and Dee Menagh
All rights reserved. No part of this book may be reproduced or utilized
in any form or by any means, electronic or mechanical, including
photocopying, recording, or by any information storage and retrieval
system, without permission in writing from the publisher.
Inquiries should be addressed to Crown Publishers, Inc., One Park Avenue,
New York, N.Y. 10016
Printed in the United States of America
Published simultaneously in Canada by
General Publishing Company Limited

Design Consultants:
Dona Z. Meilach
Dee Menagh

Library of Congress Cataloging in Publication Data
Meilach, Dona Z.
Basketry today with materials from nature.
Bibliography: p.
Includes index.
1. Basket making.   I.   Menagh, Dee, joint
author.   II.   Title.
TT879.B3M42   746.4'1   78-27283
ISBN 0-517-53134-8
ISBN 0-517-53135-6 pbk.

CONTENTS

FOREWORD

The activity of basketmaking as a craft and art form has risen steadily in the past few years. People interested in fiber arts and in the revival of ancient craft techniques have explored the basketmaking activity of early cultures and adapted them to contemporary forms. Weavers, accustomed to manipulating flexible soft fibers in infinite ways, initiated investigation of these techniques as an adjunct to contemporary fiber forms. Little by little, exploration of the materials used in ancient and traditional containers evolved. Soon, people began to be inspired by, to emulate, and expand upon, the objects and techniques they observed.

Collaboration on this book was the logical outgrowth of the experiences and talents of the two authors. Dee Menagh had been teaching ethnic studies, weaving, and contemporary basketmaking in extended education classes offered through the San Diego Museum of Man, for several years. Her pervasive interest and research into American Indian Arts and baskets from many cultures was combined with an investigation into the materials used in traditional basketmaking. Dona Meilach had previously authored *A Modern Approach to Basketry; Macramé, Creative Design in Knotting* and several other fiber related contemporary books.

Basketry Today with Materials from Nature is offered as an ongoing expression of current activity and expanding contemporary craft interest. The techniques, along with methods for gathering and preparing the materials that you need to begin making your own baskets, are clearly developed. You will find an unprecedented wealth of examples from today's craftspeople along with baskets from traditional sources and from many parts of the world.

NOTE: Photography by Dona and Mel Meilach unless otherwise credited.

BASKETRY TODAY
WITH MATERIALS FROM NATURE

1. Weaving
2. Plaiting
3. Coiling
4. Twining
5. Pine-Needle Coiling

1 BASKETS.. NATURALLY

Baskets. How we take them for granted. We see them piled high in native markets. Truckloads are shipped into our stores from all parts of the world. There are plain and colorful baskets; most are constructed simply, and many are ingeniously designed. They range from sizes as large as laundry baskets to some that are smaller then matchboxes in so many shapes and descriptions they would seem to defy categorization. Yet even the untrained eye can soon discern that certain types of baskets can be associated with specific countries. Bright and gay woven baskets come from Mexico and the Caribbean. Many have long yarn or raffia stitches in colorful abstract floral patterns, but the designs and basket shapes vary just enough to make one country's work distinguishable from the other. Finely worked materials and intricately developed forms, sometimes shaped like animals, are made in the Orient. Classically shaped, delicately coiled or twined baskets with geometric patterns are easily attributed to American Indians. Peoples of the world always have and continue to fashion baskets that are as indigenous to their environment and culture as the clothes they wear and the languages they speak.

A study of basketmaking inevitably generates a new respect for these anonymous craftspeople from every past and present culture. For no one has yet devised a mechanical substitute for the nimble fingers that weave, coil, plait, and twine natural materials into the myriad utilitarian shapes devised for the necessities of living. Baskets

A coiled basket with a handled lid. Made with beach grass by Theresa Kanrilak. Eskimo, 1976. *Courtesy: U.S. Department of the Interior, Indian Arts and Crafts Board*

have not fallen prey to mass-production methods as have most products in our culture. Plastic replicas of baskets, made by mold processes, have inundated the marketplace, and these have satisfied our utilitarian requirements.

Currently, a revival of interest and appreciation of handmade baskets have permeated the public consciousness. The sheer variety, naturalness and beauty of baskets have made them a delightful addition for interior decorating. On a scholarly level, basketmaking is rapidly gaining attention as a too long neglected activity that represents the creativity of various cultures. Collectors, and museum curators particularly, have plunged into a search for outstanding, representative baskets of ancient and modern cultures. Anthropologists emphasize that it is difficult to chronicle ancient activity in basketmaking because the vegetable fibers of which baskets are made are highly perishable. However, numerous prehistory and early-history artifacts and evidence have survived in arid caves, tombs and other favorable environments. They bear out the premise that basketmaking is among the oldest and most nearly universal crafts of primitive man.

A variety of woven baskets in different shapes are piled in an Ecuadorian marketplace, some plain, some with a stripe around them. The people's hats are also woven of a finer material than that used for the baskets and in different shapes. The techniques used for weaving baskets, hats, mats, shoes or other objects are basically the same.

Archaeological research into the basketmaking activity of every culture would take a lifetime, perhaps more. Some early research has been reprinted recently, but there are still many voids to be filled. The classic volume for basic basketry is Otis T. Mason's *Aboriginal Indian Basketry* (originally published in 1902, reprinted 1970); it is also titled *Aboriginal American Basketry* in some editions. The depth and presentation of this research have been a substantial aid to the study of man's use for and the structure of baskets.

Several new publications generated by and for the new wave of basketmaking enthusiasm appeared in the early 1970s along with the increased interest in all fiber crafts. Weaving, macramé, braiding, and a general revival in the artistic potential of manipulated fibers and fabrics fired the imaginations of serious craftspersons and hobbyists. They began to create baskets with readily available, easily workable materials used for other crafts. They discovered how easy and satisfying it was to make a basket form by coiling or twining with commercially prepared natural materials such as jute, sisal, wool and linen and with the synthetic rayon and nylon cords. These materials could be readily and imaginatively manipulated without any further preparation. They could be made into marvelous baskets that did not have to be functional. They could be outright expressive and decorative so long as our mass-production society provided enough other objects for functional containers.

As the craft of basketmaking gained attention and admiration, the activity spread across the country into the art-craft classroom, the hobby-handcraft market, and adult education programs. Many people began to delve deeper into the study of traditional basketry of other cultures, to study the construction, shaping and materials used. The variety to be observed was incredible. Form was usually dictated by function. To primitive peoples, baskets were a matter of survival. They were involved with a baby's birth, a person's life and his death. A baby was slung in a papoose frame or carried in a woven bassinet or cradle. Baskets were used for gathering and preparing grain, for fishing, for bringing home a hunted animal to be used for food. At death, a person's remains were carried, buried or cremated in a mortuary basket. No matter what form the basket took or what it was used for, the materials were gathered and prepared by the people from their indigenous plants and trees. These materials were held together by similar techniques throughout the world.

The study of traditional basketmaking activity of primitive peoples reveals that often the act of gathering and preparing the roots, branches, stems and other plant parts used to make baskets was shrouded in ritual. Many people who had learned basketmaking techniques with commercially made fibers became fascinated by the variety of natural fibers used. They wondered how and why baskets made by peoples from Africa to Newfoundland and around the globe were alike or different. In our industrialized society, going directly to nature for one's materials became an enticing endeavor. Teachers and students, workshop leaders, avid naturalists, environmentalists and botanists began to walk in the marshlands to gather grasses, trek through woods to find freshly fallen twigs, to pull dried leaves from trees and runners from vines. Old bathtubs and large aluminum pails were turned into soaking bins for the raw materials as people learned how to use them for baskets.

Though the structures of baskets proved relatively simple to analyze and emulate, the materials, their sources and preparation were not so easy. There is a vast amount of natural material available in every climate with enough different characteristics to boggle the mind. Consider that almost one quarter of the earth's plants are grasses that grow in limitless varieties in every climate where they can survive. Such grasses have been used to make coiled baskets as well as a staggering variety of other objects from toys to bridges, from boats to shelters.

Palm, one of the most widely used materials for woven mats, clothing, utensils, roofs as well as baskets, grows in an estimated 1,500 varieties in many climates. But the characteristics of only one type of palm tree may differ depending on the climate in which it is grown; the time of the year the leaves, fruit or bark are gathered can also result in different working characteristics. Even in one small locale, from one part of an island to another, the people may identify the same tree by a different name and use the parts for different purposes and in different ways.

An analysis of the trees, grasses, roots and vines used for basketmaking would be a lifelong study, a formidable task. In his book on Indian baskets, Mr. Mason states:

"Since the year 1890 a few botanists . . . have turned their attention to the plants used by the aborigines and have made new records with definite identifications of the plants concerned, covering among other subjects of Indian activity, that of basketry."

When the chapter was prepared for his book, he noted:

"When . . . the compilation of existing records was begun it was found that the earlier publications contained much that was indefinite, considerable that was incorrect, and a little that was both correct and exact."

A plaited basket in use in a South American market.

Basketry Today with Materials from Nature does not pretend to be a comprehensive, indisputable source of past and future basketmaking. Rather, it is offered as an introduction, a stimulus, an inspiration, for the contemporary craftsperson who wants to delve more deeply into the materials and the potential forms from an artistic-creative viewpoint. At best, it is necessary to generalize about the gathering and preparation of nature's materials and to urge you to experiment with those available in your community. We offer our own experiences and research. We also offer the experiences of botanists and naturalists interviewed and the notes of craftspeople who have contributed a potpourri of empirical knowledge in a spirit of exchange. With this information you will learn how and where to begin, where to look for usable materials, and broad categories for gathering, preparing and using them.

Let your inquisitiveness guide you to other resources such as articles and books on basketmaking, and on plants and trees of your area. Also investigate the nature museums in your vicinity and any displays on botany in specialized exhibits and libraries.

As you research basketmaking, you'll discover that terms differ in the writings in a manner that is often frustrating, to say the least. "Weaving" and "plaiting" may be defined as the same or different procedures in many books. Wickerwork is often called a technique though it is the material, rather than the method, which is actually weaving. "Twining" is often called "weaving." "Coiling" may be referred to as "coil binding," "rod coiling" or "bunching." The working elements may be called rods, spokes or warp; the uprights may be called weavers and weft. Sometimes the elements are simply referred to as horizontals and verticals.

We have attempted to sort out some of these terms, to make them as simple—yet as universal—as possible. We have tried to clarify, rather than contribute to the confusion. But we are not so naïve as to expect one hundred percent of the people to agree with us.

We hope that there will be agreement, however, in the theory that what you create and how you feel about it is more important than the terms used and the names given to the materials. So long as you know what you are doing and how you are working, you are the only person you have to satisfy.

Long grasses made into huge bundles are stacked and dried in preparation for basketmaking. Several baskets can be seen in the foreground. Photographed at Zagora, Southern Morocco.

2 MATERIALS— WHAT, HOW, WHERE

Ask a craftsperson where to buy jute for knotting, clay for ceramics, findings for jewelry, wood for carving, and you will probably get ready answers. The most obvious is to check your telephone book's classified pages, find the store, then purchase your needs. Ask the same people where to find natural materials for basketmaking, and you will probably be greeted with blank stares. Your phone book will be some help, but not much.

Materials from nature are as close as a potted ivy in your living room, grasses and trees in your garden, yet to think of such plants as having "function" other than decoration is almost an anachronism. Everything we use seems to be prepared, prepackaged, pre-something or other that negates a natural condition.

But it is exactly that "naturalness," that back-to-the-earth movement, that is grasping people's imaginations. It has sent them seeking, experimenting with, and learning about the materials they have available, free and plentiful.

These very qualities have made the craft universal and timeless. George Wharton James in his classic book *Indian Basketry* writes: "It would be a most interesting study, had one the time to devote to it, to see how change of environment has affected the basketry of any one tribe or race of people."

Studies of basketmakers and their environments can yield fascinating theories. Some anthropologists suggest that American Indians, for example, selected their dwelling places according to the plentitude of good basketry materials, though

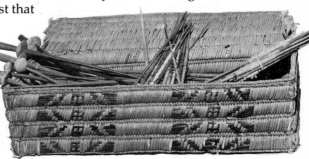

A Peruvian workbasket (about A.D.1100). Intricate, sophisticated weaving and plaiting patterns appear in existing baskets that are centuries old and from many cultures.

often one tribe used only a few of the native materials in an area. Other anthropologists support the opposing viewpoint that the people experimented with and adapted the materials that were available and continued to work with them.

Regardless of the theory, evidence indicates that basketmaking trades flourished in areas where applicable materials were available. Palm and bamboo baskets came from countries where those plants were abundant. Willow baskets were plentiful from climates where willows grew. Oak and ash splint baskets were indigenous to regions where those trees were native.

Such was the situation historically; however, such identification by plant and locale is no longer valid. In addition to the plants we gather in our homes, yards, prairies and other growing places, prepared materials imported from other countries are readily available. People in the United States, Canada, Europe, Australia and other industrialized societies can purchase bundles of reed, raffia, rattan, cane and more esoteric plants

Commercially prepared materials available from craft suppliers and applicable to natural basketry include, *from top, clockwise*: braided palm, plied sea grass, two bundles of cane, raffia and, in the center, round reed.

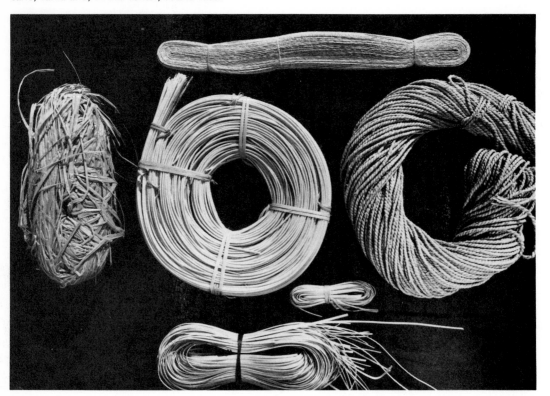

bundles of grasses gathered and sold by other natives so that he doesn't have to take time for the gathering and preparation processes.

You may wish to begin your explorations of basketmaking with natural materials sold in craft shops, such as reed, rattan, sea grass and whatever else you can find. Or you may wish to gather all materials yourself. You may also combine those you buy with those you gather. Some craftspeople plant and cultivate the growth of specific materials so they will have an abundant supply each year. One woman writes that she has a place staked out in a neighborhood prairie for a specific plant. She gathers the leaves early in the morning and carefully erases telltale marks that anyone has been there.

Another woman who lives near an experimental state garden has befriended the horticulturists, who save plant parts for her; they encourage her to work with plants none of them ever thought or heard of being used for basketmaking. Her baskets are invariably unique though she readily admits, "I may have to experiment and make three unsuccessful baskets for every successful one. But I have certainly learned a lot."

With so many natural materials in the world, it is difficult and confusing to know where and how to begin. To add to the dilemma, different parts of plants may be used for baskets: the stems, leaves, roots and bark.

The plants—and their parts—that are most frequently used and available in many climates are discussed to help simplify your introduction to natural materials. In addition, a chart of plants and information about them will be found in chapter 9. Not all plants are available in all regions of the country, so you are encouraged to experiment and make up your own working chart for materials you do have.

You will soon realize that there is an incredible variety available. The first time you pull a leaf from a plant, you may look at it in complete bewilderment and wonder, What am I going to do with it?

The answer? You are going to gather more like it, let them dry, then wet them, prepare them and make baskets with them.

Some people prefer to find two or more usable plants, become thoroughly familiar with their working potential and cultivate them for continuous use the following year, gathering the parts, drying them and having them available throughout the nongrowing seasons. "Cultivating" may involve cutting back a particular willow in the fall and keeping it free of underbrush so that the long branches can complete their growth the following year. Long willow branches make beautiful cores for coiled baskets and weavers for woven baskets. It might involve keeping a plant under control so it will be easy to harvest.

Generally, the *what, how, where* for natural materials are:

1   COLLECTING

FRESH MATERIALS

Select fresh green materials and carefully cut or pull them from the plant, being very careful not to interfere with annual growth process or plant appearance. Always leave more than you remove so as not to destroy a plant or an area. Generally, take fresh parts in the spring and fall from shrubs and woody plants because there is a minimal amount of sap flowing compared with the more active summer growth periods. Always take the portions at the growth joint the same way you might properly prune a plant. Use sharp cutting tools and do not rip or tear leaves, branches or bark.

DRIED MATERIALS

Collect dried materials by gathering those that have fallen onto the ground from trees or gently pulling off dried leaves from the bottom of the plant just before the plant would normally shed them.

For information about plant growth periods, cutting and pruning methods and so forth, refer to garden books that identify and describe the plants in your area. Write to your State Department of Conservation to learn about laws that protect local plant life. Be very cautious so as not to take any plant parts from controlled areas such as National and State Parks, where removing even a dried branch is prohibited.

2 DRYING

Fresh materials are usually, but not always, dried before they are worked. They are dried by exposing them to the air so they don't mildew. Place freshly picked green materials in single layers on screening or newspaper, and cover them with papers or brown bags with holes punched so the air can circulate through and around them. Place them in a garage, basement or other airy place. Fresh materials dried by this method will retain much of their natural color as opposed to drying them in direct sunlight. Those that are dried in direct sunlight tend to lose their color as they would if they were dried outdoors naturally.

The drying process you select will depend on the colors and texture you want. You will have to experiment. You may wish to establish a "control": Dry one group of the gathered materials indoors and another outdoors and observe the difference. Perhaps both can be combined in one basket for an interesting departure for contemporary designs.

Fresh materials can be worked and then allowed to dry. There is a tendency for the materials to shrink as they dry, and the basket structure becomes loose. But often the procedure is satisfactory with good results.

Some species of plants—such as yuccas, for example—yield beautiful baskets if they are picked partially dry and exposed to dew or rain until the subtle color differences and textures are reached. Much depends on when the plant parts are picked. It all requires experimentation and experience.

Traveling in farm and back areas of many countries where basket-making is a native industry, you can observe bundles of plant parts drying outside, within a living space, or in lean-tos and barns. Drying time can vary from a few days to several months. Once the plants are dried, they can be stored indefinitely until they are ready for use.

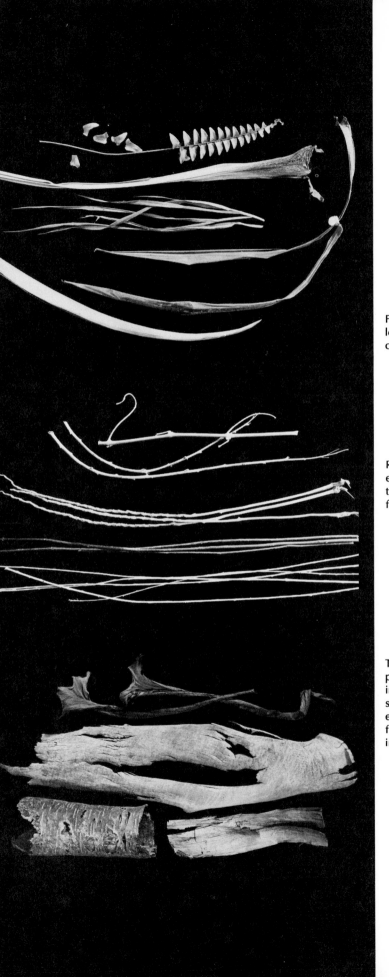

Flat materials perfect for baskets would be leaves from such plants as the fern, dracaena, cattail, flax and palm.

Round materials can be found among a variety of plants from small shrubs to large trees that grow in almost every area. They include flexible twigs, branches, stems and stalks.

The outer bark and casings from trees and plants can be incorporated into basket forms in their entirety or when they are stripped and split. Shown are philodendron sheaths, eucalyptus, birch bark and a piece of bark from an unidentified tree that was picked up in the woods.

3   WETTING AND OTHER PREPARATIONS

Dried plant materials are usually brittle and tend to crack or break; they lose their strength and flexibility. These lost qualities, which must exist to make them workable, are restored by wetting. Thin, fine materials may be lightly dipped in water before using. Heavier, more fibrous plant parts may require soaking for hours, overnight or for several days. A good rule of thumb is the woodier the material, the longer the wetting time. Test the material by gently bending it; when it is flexible and will not crack, it is ready for use.

Wrap the wet materials in a dampened towel to absorb excess moisture from leaves or branches so they don't become waterlogged. This practice also keeps the materials from drying out and becoming brittle again. Any dampened material that will not be used within about 24 hours should be allowed to redry, then dampened again before using. Materials that are kept damp too long may become mildewed and rot. Do not store materials in plastic bags for the same reason.

Other types of preparation—in addition to dampening—may require splitting of logs, trimming protrusions from twigs and branches, cutting leaf ends and stripping them. Roots should be washed, soaked and trimmed. Some plants require boiling to remove bark and to break down the fibers so that branches or twigs, for instance, may be peeled and scraped easily. You'll find specific procedures described and discussed in the various chapters and demonstrations.

Remember that the study and use of natural materials is an ongoing learning process. You are urged to constantly refer to botany books, books and pamphlets about Indian basketry and those from other native

Cattail and palm leaves are soaked in a large tub in preparation for use. They will be transferred onto a wet towel, which will absorb excess moisture and keep them damp.

cultures. The preparation of bamboo by the Japanese, for example, can be applied to other kinds of supple trees and their parts. Entire books have been written on single plants and the possible uses of all the parts of one tree. Actual plant technology can only be touched on here as an introduction to the use of natural materials. Your readings will reveal that the best ways for working certain materials have been determined by various groups of people. Often they are rigidly adhered to in an almost ritualistic manner, always the same, never varying. These cultural facts can be found in readings of the American Indians, Africans, Oceanic peoples and so forth; they offer a wealth of information for the modern craftsperson.

THE SEARCH

Each type of natural material has its own unique uses and limitations. Prepared cane, reed and plied cords such as sea grass, jute and sisal are available in long lengths that can be woven in an uninterrupted fashion. Branches, leaves, roots and grasses gathered outdoors are relatively short; they require piecing, starting and stopping so they must be used more judiciously. Generally, try to collect pieces that are as long as possible.

You may want to wear gloves, long-sleeved shirts and long pants when you gather plants to minimize scratches and insect bites.

Different species of pine trees yield needles of assorted lengths, textures, colors and diameters. Gather the fallen needles from the ground or take fresh needles carefully from the tree. (See chapter 7.)

Dried branches from a dead tree, about to be felled, will provide abundant round materials for baskets.

Always examine the plants you collect for insects or larvae and treat them with a garden insecticide before drying and storing. Another suggestion is to put gathered materials in plastic bags and place these in a freezer overnight as a precaution against insects living and multiplying in the plant materials. (But do not "store" in plastic bags.)

Before you begin gathering, it is wise to categorize materials as those that are *flat* and *round* and by the general preparation methods required and uses for them. Among the easiest to find, the most versatile and reliable, are:

FLAT MATERIALS

Leaves—Cattails or other varieties of bulrushes grown in marshy areas. Palm, yucca, flax and other long, broad leaves can be used whole or stripped into narrow lengths. Day-lily leaves (available throughout the country) may be used flat or twisted.

Leaf Sheaths—Such as philodendron. Pick when dry and separated from the leaf. Use flat, stripped or twisted.

Bark—Peel dried bark from trees; pick it up from the ground. Birch,

Cattails grow at the edges of marshy areas. Dee Menagh looks for long, narrow leaves, the longer the better. Some varieties may grow as high as 9 feet tall.

The stem of the palm frond can be split and the entire branch separated into two parts with the leaves intact on each part. Each half can be used for a variety of shapes.

Individual palm leaves are split for use as long, thin weavers. These are removed from the stem.

eucalyptus, yew. Use split for flat elements. Use portions for adding to other techniques.

Pods, Husks—Catalpa, cornhusks.

ROUND MATERIALS

Branches and Twigs from many varieties of broad-leaf trees and shrubs such as willow, elder, birch, elm and others.

Stems and Stalks from rushes, grasses and ferns; the flower stems from the palm; bunched grass used in groups for coiling.

Roots from cattail, sugar pine, cedar, red fir. Sugar-pine roots may be cut into slender strands used for weaving.

Vines—Select the long runners for weaving and for the core of coiling. Trim off the leaves.

Pine Needles—The longer the better for easy handling. Use for pine-needle coiled baskets.

Reed—Commercially prepared and available in skeins.

Sea Grass, Jute, Sisal, Coconut and Other Plied Materials in various diameters. Available commercially.

Splints—*Ash, Oak, Hickory, Elm* and others are stripped from the inner bark of cut logs. Such logs may have been felled for lumber or land clearance. Or buy processed woods.

Cane—Available commercially.

Raffia—Available commercially. Use for weaving, sewing, coiling.

Fresh and dried leaves of the flax can be taken from the lower part of the plant. Select long, broad leaves.

The dried sheath from a new philodendron leaf can be pulled away from the plant easily. Large varieties of the plant have long, broad, beautifully textured sheaths that can be flattened after wetting, cut into strips and used for weaving and plaiting.

The dried, leathery-looking leaves of aloe plants are excellent flat materials for basketmaking. Pull them from under the new growth.

The aloe arborescens grows outdoors in warm climates and can be cultivated indoors in cool climates. Saw-toothed leaves are sharp. Use gloves to gather.

Wild grasses with long round stems are favorites of basketmakers around the world and have been used by every culture where they grow.

Use a heavy clipper to cut thick branches.

17

Ivy, vines and other long, trailing houseplants can supply round weaving elements when the leaves are stripped from the stems.

Outdoor ivy is usually thicker and heavier than indoor varieties and yields longer, sturdier and woodier stems. Simply pick up the vines and cut them; they regenerate quickly.

Palm fiber—a fabriclike growth around the trunk of the coconut palm and other varieties—can be readily pulled away from the lower part of the tree without any damage to the tree.

The long leaves of the dracaena draco tree have beautifully shaped and colored stem ends that are favored by contemporary basketmakers. Dried leaves should be pulled from the lower part of the plant. Select them as long and broad as possible because they can be cut and stripped into narrow weaving elements. (See Demonstration, page 32.)

The flower stalk from a palm tree has a unique texture and design. It is a round element that is especially attractive and easy to use in baskets. It grows as shown at left. Stalks may be easily gathered from low growing trees or from fallen fronds that have been blown down by the winds.

Stems are removed from the flower stalk.

MAKING SPLINTS

Thin splints used for basketmaking are made from the inner bark of young trees. Many Indian tribes used white oak, hickory, apple, white or black ash, sometimes hazel, elm or poplar. Much depended on the availability of the young, straight trees.

The Indian tradition of splint basketry remains strong and traditional among today's tribes, and the practice has been emulated by craftsmen throughout Appalachia. The beauty and individuality of splint baskets, especially those of the Cherokee Indians of the Qualla Indian Boundary of North Carolina, have made them collector's items whether old or new. Contemporary Cherokee Indian women often help support their families with their craft. They are free to create new patterns and sign their names to their creations.

Elsie Watty, well known for her quality, beautifully crafted baskets, shared her techniques with us. These techniques could be applied to baskets made by peoples anywhere in either a traditional or contemporary mode.

Splints may be made from the trees in the procedure described. Flat splints can be purchased commercially. Other flat materials that simulate traditional wood splints may be substituted.

The young trees with trunks from 3- to 10-inch diameters are cut in 4-foot lengths. The log is cut into quarter sections.

The outer annual ring portion (a), next to the inner bark, is used for making splints. There is an almost invisible growth layer between these annual layers.

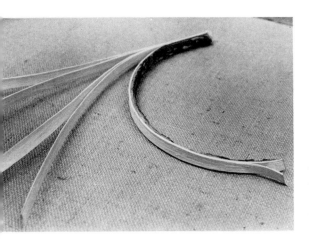

The layers are split and separated to achieve the splints with a uniform thickness. A penknife is a good tool for splitting. The splints are pulled apart as the knife is edged down between the ring layers (see page 22).

The splints are further prepared by cutting them to a uniform width and scraping them smooth with a sharp knife just as you might scrape a carrot. Some of the natural-color splints will be sanded or planed to prepare them for a dyebath. Soaking opens the pores so the dye will be absorded. The dye made of brown walnut root gives the basket a contrasting tone.

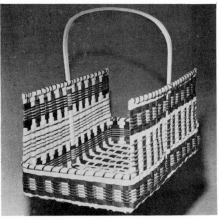

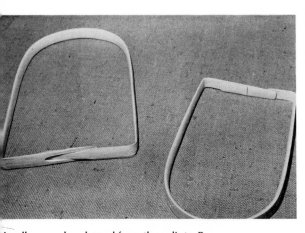

Handles are also shaped from the splints. Portions are hand carved as needed for the final design but with emphasis on the support function required.

A finished Cherokee Indian basket by Elsie Watty. Observe how the handle is woven around and through the basket's sides and bottom. *Series photographed at the Members' Gallery of Qualla Arts and Crafts Mutual, Inc., Cherokee, North Carolina, with special permission from the U.S. Department of the Interior, Indian Arts and Crafts Board.*

Ballard Jenkins demonstrates the traditional approach for using splints to make a woven basket . . . called "splintwork." *Above:* White oak splints are prepared, as shown on pages 20–21. Thick splints have to be split further so all are even, uniformly thin and flexible.

Above right:
He uses a sharp knife to split the thick splint at the edge . . .

. . . then carefully pulls each side of the splint apart.

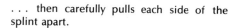

He begins the base with 8 strips to yield 8 spokes (16 ends). One spoke (beneath his hand) is split to make a total of 17, the uneven number necessary for weaving. The weaver (weft) is narrower and thinner than the spokes (warp). All the elements have been dampened for working.

A variety of finished baskets by Ballard Jenkins, some with and some without handles. Observe the different border treatments.

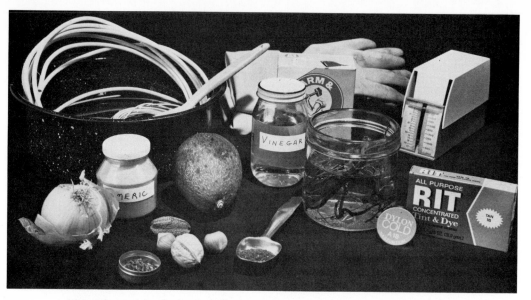

Materials used for dyeing include prepared commercial dyes or those you glean from roots, bark, nutshells, berries, onionskins, turmeric, saffron, tea, and so forth. Cream of tartar, vinegar, salt and baking soda are mordants used to set the dyes. Glass or enamel pans are best for boiling the plant materials in the dyebath. You will also need a wooden spoon, rubber gloves, a household scale, and materials for straining the solutions.

DYEING NATURAL MATERIALS

The process of coloring or dyeing natural materials could easily be the subject for an entire book. From the beginning of time, the making of dyes has been an empirical endeavor. Plant parts used for dyeing include berries, roots, leaves and bark. Their availability differs by locale. The colors they yield differ according to the time of year they are picked, how they are prepared and so forth. Among early cultures, formulas were usually not written; in fact, they were often zealously guarded so others would not duplicate what had been found by tedious trial and error.

Today, using natural substances for coloring basket material remains an experimental process, though one can get fairly reasonable results from some of the easier-to-find materials such as walnut hulls and leaves, onionskins, elderberries, eucalyptus bark, hickory bark, tea leaves, beets and similar plant parts. Generally, books on dyeing yarns (listed in the Bibliography) will lead you to assorted plants that may be available in your region and be applicable to basketry materials. You will have to gather and experiment with them for the specific materials you are dyeing.

It is simple, time-consuming, but, when successful, very gratifying to extract dye color from plants. Barks and roots generally should be dried, pulverized, then soaked overnight. Cover them with water and simmer until the water is a color you would like to impart to the plants you have prepared for your baskets. Strain the dye material from the water; place the plant material in the water and simmer for a few minutes—the length of time will depend on the material you are dyeing and its thickness and porosity. Woody materials such as ash splints should be soaked before placing in the dyebath so as to open the pores to accept the dye color. After dyeing, the grain may be raised, and splints will have to be sanded and smoothed before being used for a basket.

Onionskins, berries, blossoms, twigs and leaves should be covered

Japanese bamboo flower basket woven of wide and narrow strips. *Photographed at The Gallery, Palos Verdes Estates, California*

Traditional baskets—new and old—from various cultures may be studied for a multitude of ideas: shaping, color usage, materials and detailing of handles and attachments, weave progressions, and so forth.

Dracaena Draco leaf spokes with twining of handspun mohair and wools. By Dee Menagh.

Flax twined over stalks of the palm seed frond. By Augusta Lucas-Andreae. *Courtesy artist*

Melon-shaped basket using a variety of natural materials including elm twigs, rattan, date plum seed stems, philodendron sheaths, coconut palm fiber. By Carolyn Thom.

Melon-shaped baskets. White ash spokes are twined with split cane for the larger basket. The smaller one is made completely of white ash splints. By Rosemary Randall. *Photo: Dee Menagh*

Twig basket. Half round reed woven over round reed. *Collection Max Lenderman*

Orange-tipped *Dracaena Draco* leaf spokes twined with New Zealand flax. By Myrna Brunson.

Twined buckthorn twigs over willow twigs. By Dorothy Gill Barnes. *Courtesy artist*

Sewn, padded, and quilted palm fiber box. By Ann Dunn.

Container. A basic form has been shaped using a variety of materials including twigs, woven mat parts, wire, and wool. Adobe was added over the entire piece. By Dale Gaynor. *Photo: Dale D. Menagh*

May basket. Double-crocheted colored raffia. By Shirley Sestric-Friedlander.

Coiled pine needles (detail of a sculpture in Chapter 7) sewn with raffia and combined with shaped copper sheet. By Carol Goss. *Courtesy artist*

Coiled pine needles sewn with cotton thread. Guinea hen feathers added. By Dee Menagh.

Ash splints plaited on the bottom, then shaped and twined with waxed linen and nylon. By B. J. Adams. *Photo: Clark Adams*

Assorted basket shapes from Bali. Observe the various designs and varieties of indigenous materials . . . some natural and some dyed.

Soft shaped basket from Ecuador made of sisal using the special looping method illustrated in Chapter 8.

Wicker tray. By Hopi Indians. Twined. Dyed split yucca leaves. *Collection San Diego Museum of Man, San Diego, California*

Woven splints with "twist" detail. By Winnebago Indians. *Collection Field Museum of Natural History, Chicago, Illinois. Photo: George DiSylvestro*

Plaited basket of natural and dyed splints. By Cherokee Indians of the Qualla Indian Boundary of North Carolina.

Detail showing the color, weave, and handle attachment of a plaited basket by the Cherokee Indians of the Qualla Indian Boundary of North Carolina.

Tagine basket. Morocco. Coiled grasses with raffia. Leather strips are overlaid for decoration. The top is leather.

Willow branch spokes twined with stripped yucca leaves. Eucalyptus seed pods are added over the spoke endings. By Linda Anderson.

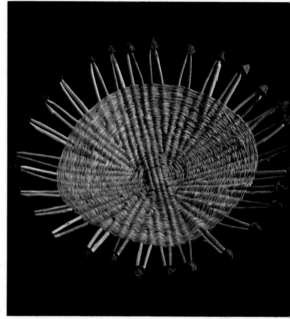

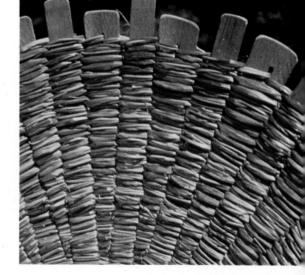

Twined basket (detail) of iris leaves and grass over mahogany wood spokes. By Dorothy Gill Barnes. *Courtesy artist*

with water and simmered. Berries and leaves should be mashed when softened to release the juice that yields the dye color. Strain the materials from the colored water, then place the plants to be dyed in the water and simmer. Mordants, chemical aids for setting the colors, will vary, but they include alum, chrome, tin, cream of tartar, vinegar and salt. These should be noted when working with the formulas given for dyeing yarns and fabrics. Refer to the chart on page 193.

SYNTHETIC DYES

Prepared, packaged dyes purchased from a store are easier to use and possibly more reliable than those you extract from plants. Yet they, too, require experimentation because of the vagaries and varieties of plants to be dyed. There are different families of synthetic dyes that can be used on various plant materials:

Household dyes consist of a mixture of basic, acid and other dyestuffs for use on a general range of fiber mixtures. They usually require hot water, which can be detrimental to delicate plants.

Fiber-Reactive Dyes can be used in cooler water mixtures and may prove more permanent than the household dyes on some materials.

At best, it is necessary to be vague about any specific formulas for dyeing plants. Our own experiments have ranged from abortive to excellent with several given recipes including those gleaned from American Indian sources. Comparing those that appear in other books indicates that every writer has been able to give results based on his own experimentation. When we have tried them, they worked sometimes on some plants. The same range resulted when the formulas were tried in classroom situations with many students.

When preparing dyes for natural materials, we urge you to consult books on Indian basketry and those using dyes for fabrics.

Many types of roots, cut into pieces, are immersed in a dyebath. They yield a coloring for use with natural ash splints and other materials.

Natural color ash splints, combined with some that have been colored, were woven for the basket, *right*.

SHAPING PROCEDURES

Good basket shapes do not happen haphazardly—most baskets are worked over a shape. A basketmaker's workshop may have huge carved forms of wood for large oval baskets or those with rounded bottoms. You can improvise forms from blocks of wood glued or nailed together, as shown; a box or a round, oval or rectangular object that is easy to work over.

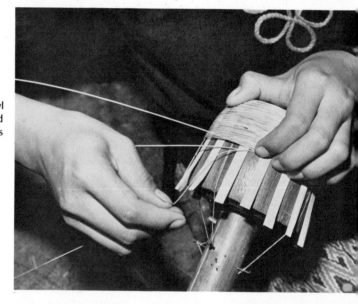

A Thailand basketmaker develops a bowl shape over a rounded wood form supported by a pole. Strings wound around the nails hold interchangeable forms to the pole.

A hat is woven on a specifically shaped wooden form. Materials are almost always woven while slightly damp.

KEEPING RECORDS AND SAMPLES

Margaret Henderson keeps an organized record of her basketry experience. A sample of each material is snipped and labeled with all necessary information such as when and where the plant was gathered, how it was handled and any other pertinent data. The materials used in one basket are placed in a plastic bag and assembled into a notebook, as shown. Dye information can be recorded on a card or a sheet of notes placed with a photo of the basket for future reference.

CLEANING, PRESERVING, REPAIRING

Natural materials can be perishable and, depending on what has been used, quite fragile. Even those we think of in terms of heavy usage, of carrying large loads, will endure only for a relatively short time unless they are properly taken care of. Although the baskets you make will not be used on the backs of laden donkeys, or for carrying vegetables to and from the marketplace, they do require some basic care to keep them beautiful for a long time.

Clean baskets by gently brushing dust away with a soft-bristled paintbrush. If the baskets should require washing, spray them lightly with water from a flower mister, the kitchen faucet or a softly controlled garden hose, and let them air-dry. Try to handle the baskets with two hands rather than picking them up by the rims, which is a weak part of the structure.

In the past, baskets were sometimes varnished to preserve them and give them shine, but museum curators frown on this practice today. They feel that the natural materials must be allowed to "breathe."

Repairing and restoring baskets is a formidable task. It is virtually impossible to match plant materials in type, color and texture. There are very few people who can do it.

3 WEAVING

Weaving, one of the basic procedures for fashioning materials into baskets, is essentially the same technique today that it has been for countless years. Many of us became familiar with the weaving process in grade school when we "wove" strips of paper for placemats or cloth for potholders. Some of us learned to weave reed in Scout groups as we tried to appreciate and emulate the crafts of our ancestors. Usually there was no need to pursue the craft of weaving because an abundance of woven manufactured products was ever present to satisfy needs.

The weaving process for basketmaking is so simple that almost everyone who tries it can do it immediately. The weavers (weft) are carried under and over the spokes (warp) in the basic tabby weave illustrated in the demonstration on page 32. Natural materials can create a problem initially only because we are not as accustomed to handling them as we are long yarns or ropes. Leaves, branches and roots are relatively short and require constant piecing, or they may seems stiff and stubborn. With a little patience, practice and experience most people quickly learn to manipulate the materials as naturally, as confidently, as though they had been doing it all their lives.

Making a first basket with a new technique and new materials should be considered a learning experience, a sampler. One experienced craftswoman says, "Actually I consider every basket an 'experiment' no matter how many I have made because of the constant variables of nature's materials. This is part of the challenge and the fun."

Warrior's shield. Africa. Approx. 24 inches high, 18 inches wide. The woven strips have reinforcing branches in the center under the warp. The entire form is laced to a supportive piece of shaped bark. *Collection: Field Museum of Natural History, Chicago. Photo: Dee Menagh*

Materials from nature used for weaving can be conveniently broken down into "flat" and "round" materials; each type requires a different mode of working. We show you approaches to both in the accompanying demonstrations.

For "flat" materials use wood or paper splints and prebraided grasses available from your craft supplier. You may wish to gather fresh rushes, cattail, dracaena, palm, flax or other flat leaves. Dry them and soak them, as described in chapter 2. Use hard, sturdy materials for spokes, and thin, long supple leaves for weavers.

For "round" materials you may begin with easily available reed, rattan, bamboo and sea grass from a craft supplier. For fresh materials, gather twigs, branches, roots, vines and grasses for bunching.

Always prepare all materials, fresh and commercial, by properly dampening or soaking them before you begin. CAREFUL PREPARATION is the KEY to a successful experience. Too often, beginners are so enthusiastic, so anxious to work and to see quick results, that they try materials when they are dry. They become quickly discouraged should the splints crack or the twigs snap. Basketmaking takes time, patience . . . and preparation.

A finished woven basket will usually be stiff, sturdy and very durable, which accounts for its popularity. The weaving is most often developed from the center bottom and worked upward. You can recognize a woven basket by its distinctive beginning and the progression of the spokes (warp) and weavers (weft). The basic weaves are illustrated along with alternatives for beginning to weave and procedures for developing the shapes, designs and finishes.

Almost any shape basket—round, square, oval or free form—can be accomplished by weaving. Occasionally, a basket will not shape the way you expect or want it to because of the vagaries and "will" of the natural materials. You may be able to join with nature; try dipping the form in water and reshaping and holding it to the desired shape with string,

Woven baskets in an Ecuadorian market illustrate some of the possible shapes and sizes that can be created with flat materials using only the simple tabby weave.

Woven and plaited baskets finished and in progress. Designs, materials and shapes are typical of traditional baskets of southeastern United States.

rubber bands or fabric strips tied around it until the materials dry. Or you can let nature have her way and possibly develop a basket that is so uniquely shaped it will be a prizewinner wherever it is shown. Additional suggestions for achieving patterns, color and surface embellishments into the woven basket are shown in the chapters on plaiting (4) and twining (5). Most of the procedures for these techniques are adaptable and interchangeable with one another.

Whether you wish to weave traditional basket forms or work in a modern mode, the choice is yours. Whichever you select, be inventive and innovative with the materials, letting them suggest ideas to you as often as you try to impose your creative will upon them.

Lidded baskets made by the Winnebago Indians may be studied by the contemporary basketmaker for their color, variations as to how the weavers are placed, handle designs, and attachments.

BASIC WOVEN BASKETS

The basic "tabby weave," also called "plain weave," consists of bringing the horizontal weavers (warp) *over one* and *under one* of each of the spokes (weft). Uneven numbers of spokes are required so that the under and over progression alternates in each row to result in the woven "fabric."

Another weaving pattern results when the weavers are carried *over two* and *under two* spokes. This pattern is called "twill weave." Interspersing plain weave with twill and other progressions of over and under may be used to give the final surface texture variety and interest.

To begin a woven basket with natural materials, dampen 4 dracaena draco leaves to be used for spokes. Trim off the ends and cut each leaf through the middle lengthwise to result in 8 relatively even widths. This simple gradual shape can easily be evolved without a form.

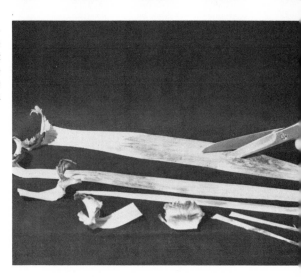

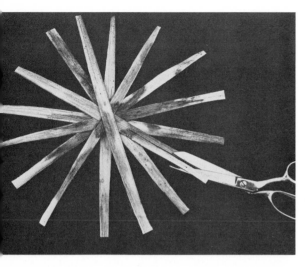

Lay 2 leaves so they crisscross one another and continue adding the others and spread evenly, as shown, to result in the 16 spoke ends. Select the widest spoke and split it down the middle to yield the uneven number of spokes needed for weaving (17).

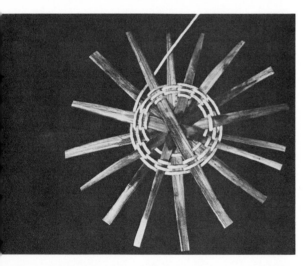

Begin weaving with a flat flexible weaver. (Here we are using commercially available braided palm that does not require dampening.) Weave 3 rows. Place a mark under the beginning spoke so you can count rows evenly and know where to begin subsequent rows. When your weaver runs out, place an end of the new length between the old length and the spoke to hide it (see page 39).

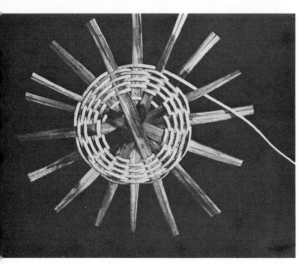

To expand the diameter of the base, weave two more rows, then split *each* spoke down the middle except one (33 working ends).

A design change may be woven into the center of the basket for interest. Take three narrow strips from dracaena draco leaves and weave them into a long braid to repeat the braid design of the palm but in another texture and color. Then add this braid for only one row. Use a clothespin to hold the braid end together until additional rows of braided palm are completed if necessary. Begin to shape the basket by pulling the weaver a little more tightly in each row to result in a shallow bowl shape.

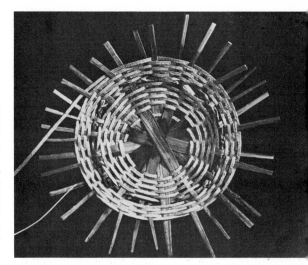

Weave additional rows until you are about one inch from the spoke ends. As you proceed, continue to pull the weaver so the bowl gradually takes shape. To end the basket and secure the weaving, fold each spoke alternating forward and backward over the woven rows.

The finished basket. By Dee Menagh.

Another good combination for weaving is split dracaena draco leaves for spokes and split flax leaves for weavers. All must be gathered. Moisten the flax leaves very well so they may be manipulated without cracking. As you weave, twist the flax leaves so they will curve; they do not have the same bias pull as the braided palm in the previous demonstration.

The weaving builds up; flax leaves are added by placing the ends of the new weavers between the spokes and the ends of the previous weavers (see page 39). This basket will be rougher in texture and more rustic than the braided palm in the preceding basket.

BASES AND HOW TO BEGIN THEM

Bases may be started by a variety of methods depending on the shape desired, the materials available, and how you wish to work them. A base diameter may be expanded by adding spokes at corners or within the basket side. Single or doubled spokes may be added as required for a specific desired shape. The same methods illustrated in the twining demonstrations (pages 86–89) are also applicable to the woven base. For all weaving, remember to split or add one spoke to yield the uneven number of spokes required.

Four spokes interwoven with four spokes yield a square base beginning.

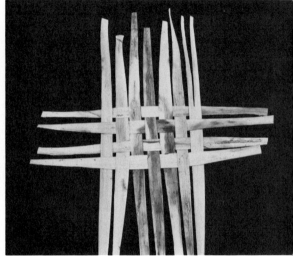

Four spokes interwoven with seven spokes will yield an oval or rectangular base.

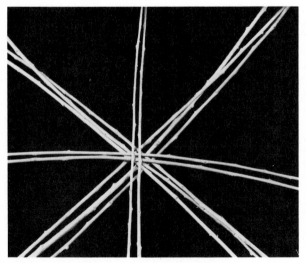

Round branches are placed *over* and *across* one another in groups rather than interweaving them. The numbers of branches used will depend on their thickness and the size of the basket you want to evolve.

Grouped crossover branches will have this appearance after they are overlaid and then woven.

Often the round elements are split and one group is placed *through* the other for a base that is less bulky than overlaid branches. Slit the elements with a sharp knife.

This base was started with slit branches for an oblong basket. Observe how the five horizontal elements are placed close together and the six verticals spaced far apart. The end spokes will be spread to yield the oval form.

Increases for shaping may be made with bent twigs and added, as shown. These increases will be incorporated into the weaving as it progresses.

Another idea for beginning a basket: Round or flat elements may be used with this method.

THE BASKET BUILDUP

Weaving procedures in the middle of the basket can vary tremendously for variety and pattern interest. This is where you can exercise your own creativity and inventiveness.

Flat dracaena draco leaves are used for spokes. Weavers, also flat dracaena draco leaves, are combined with round grasses to add interest to the body of the basket.

Dracaena draco spokes with weavers of dracaena draco are combined with round branches.

Alternate the weavers of round grasses and branches, using the flat dracaena draco leaves as spokes.

Decrease a shape by varying the number of spokes over which you weave. To pull a shape in tightly, weave over two and under two, as shown. For a more gradual decrease weave over two and under one, as needed.

To add in new weaving elements:

For flat weavers, lay a new end in back of the previous weaver end and between it and the spoke. Continue working with the new length.

For round weavers, cut each end on a slant and place them together as a splice. Sometimes the new end can be simply laid *on top of* the old end.

For a relief surface treatment, weavers can be added over existing woven strips and twisted or curled in various designs (see the demonstrations on pages 70–75). By Shereen LaPlantz.

FINISHES AND BORDERS

The basket ending must be worked so it se-
cures the weaving. A border may function
solely to hold the weaving onto the spoke;
more likely it is also decorative. There are
hundreds of borders possible for baskets . . .
we show a few of the basic, and easier-to-do,
decorative finishes. Most others are evolved
from these.

A sandwich border with a single slanted lash.
Place one element alternately in front and one
element in back of the spokes. As you work
hold the elements in place with a clothespin
or other clip. Carry the lash (split cane in this
illustration) between each spoke, over the
top, and between the next spoke, all around
the rim.

A sandwich border with a crossed lash. Make
a first row of lashing as shown at left with a
single slant. Work a second row over it to
form an X.

A folded spoke border yields a sturdy rim.
Place a flat element behind the flexible
spokes. Lash, as shown, and fold each spoke
at a 45° angle, and catch the spoke end beneath the next lash. This repeat design is attractive and functional.

Twining may be used to secure the woven
elements on round or flat, flexible or stiff,
spokes. For the twining procedures, see page
84. Here, two twined rows of sea grass secure
flat dracaena draco weavers on round spokes.

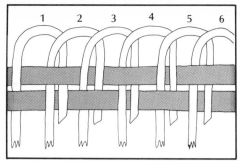

Looped Spokes: Adjacent

Take spoke 1 and insert it into the weaving to the right of spoke 2. Take spoke 2 and insert it into the weaving to the right of spoke 3. Continue with each spoke in progression around the basket to make this looped border.

The following borders are adaptable for weaving and twining. The size of the loops can be made narrow or wide depending on the number of spokes skipped for each loop. The spoke ends may be poked down into the woven or twined material. The ends can also be allowed to protrude on the inside or outside of the basket. Always trim spoke ends *after* the borders are made.

a good alternate border idea, wrap an
a element at the edge after the loops are
le.

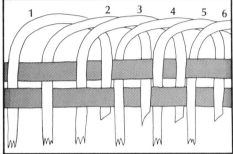

Looped Spokes: Alternating

A loop is made by placing spoke 1 behind spokes 2 and 3 and next to 4, then poking it into the weaving. Take spoke 2 and place it next to spoke 5, then take spoke 3 and place it next to spoke 6 and continue working in this method all around the edge.

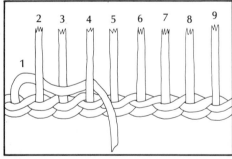

Woven Border

To make a decorative woven edge, weave the spokes in this progression:
Bring spoke 1 behind spoke 2, in front of spoke 3 and behind spoke 4. Push the end into the weaving or allow it to protrude on the inside or the outside of the basket.

edge woven with groups of four spokes.

Right: Continue . . .
Weave spoke 2 behind spoke 3, in front of spoke 4, and behind spoke 5. Repeat the steps with each spoke in order and continue around the basket until all ends are woven together. Trim the ends evenly.

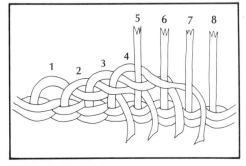

Cattail leaves were cut into strips and braided, then used for the weavers. Ends of the elements were overlapped and tied into four separate sections for a nontraditional contemporary statement. Approx. 10 inches high, 12-inch diameter. By Dorothy Gill Barnes.

Dracaena draco leaves used for spokes and weavers were woven over a wastebasket. The stem ends of the weavers were not cut off so they would be a natural embellishment when allowed to protrude from the woven surface. They have a beautiful texture and a spotted orange color. 14 inches high, 11-inch diameter. By Gertrude Wick.

Contemporary adaptation of a traditional Cherokee honeysuckle basket (1967) with an unusual detail worked into the weave around the center. Flat and round elements are combined; some have been colored with natural dyes. *Courtesy: U.S. Department of the Interior, Indian Arts and Crafts Board.*

THE MELON-SHAPE BASKET

The "melon-shape" basket, which is so called because of its similarity to the shape of the fruit, has several other nomenclatures in the history of basketmaking. Some researchers call it a "hip" basket because its weight is supported by the hip when the basket is filled with eggs or other produce. Sometimes it was called an "egg" basket because it was often used to carry eggs. Still other names for it are "rib type" and "hoop" basket because of its construction.

Materials for a melon-shape basket should be gathered and prepared about three weeks before you want to make it because the branches must be formed to hold the shapes needed for weaving them. Always collect and form extra branches should some of them break or crack. The handle and rim branches should be thicker than the spoke branches. You will need 2 long, very thick branches for the handle and rim; 3 thick branches for the spokes. These will be cut in half to make 6.

The weft may be made from additional thin branches gathered from the same type of tree as the handle and spokes or you can use splints, cattail leaves or any other flat or round materials.

All branches must be pliable either from some sap still being in them or by soaking. Wrap all the dampened branches around, or place them

Begin a melon-shape basket with two branches shaped as hoops and lashed together with a diamond-shaped warp (similar to a God's-eye). A spring clip clothespin keeps ends and parts together.

within, a round or oval bucket to hold them to the shape you want your basket to be. Leave them with this form for about 3 weeks so they will be preshaped and ready for weaving as shown in the demonstration. Observe that the diamond design that lashes the rim and handle together, and holds the spokes in place, is both decorative and functional.

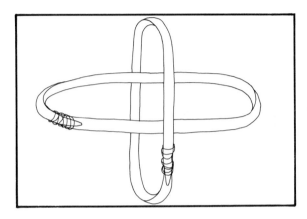

Form the rim and handle branches into a hoop by splicing the ends, overlapping and securing them with a stout string, wire, length of flax or other strong plant material. Place one hoop crosswise inside the other, as shown. The wrap with the diamond-shape design will secure the rim and handle.

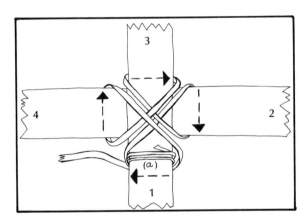

Lay the end of your weaver on top of 1 (a), and wrap it two times (only for the beginning), catching the end under the wrap to secure it.

Then wrap each spoke only once, carry the wrap on top of, behind, over to and around the next spoke in this progression:
on top of 2, behind it, over to and on top of 3
behind 3, over to and on top of 4
behind 4, over to and on top of 1
behind 1, over to and on top of 2
Continue, always placing each new length next to, *not* on top of, the preceding wrap to result in the finished example.
When the wrap shortens or breaks, tuck the old and new ends into the back rows. Tuck the final end under in the same way.

When the wraps on both sides of the basket are the desired size, begin to insert the spokes. Cut the 3 spoke branches in half and taper the ends. Space 3 of them evenly at each side of the basket, as shown. Poke the ends through the diamond wrap neatly and evenly. You now have 9 wrap elements (6 spokes + the bottom of the handle and two sides of the rim). Begin to weave in and out of the spokes with flexible materials, starting below the diamond at each handle side and working toward the center bottom. (See finished examples, pages 46–47.) Push the weavers tightly toward each end as you weave to create solidly filled in areas.

A melon-shape basket of woven willow. 1926.
13 inches high, 17 inches wide, 14 inches
deep. *Collection: Mr. and Mrs. John W.
Smith, Chicago, Illinois*

The basket frame is made of natural branches,
the woven elements are vegetable-dyed commercial reeds. Branch nodes of the frame,
and handle, are allowed to protrude. 14
inches high, about 18 inches diameter. *Collection: Max L. Lenderman, Rochester, New
York*

Flat-backed melon-shape basket of flat natural and dyed white oak splints by the Eastern band of Cherokee Indians of North Carolina.

A melon-shape basket woven of split cane with the cane also used for the God's-eye. A palm seed frond stalk with stems is used for the handle and decorative touch. 13 inches high, 13 inches diameter. By Polly Jacobs Giacchina.

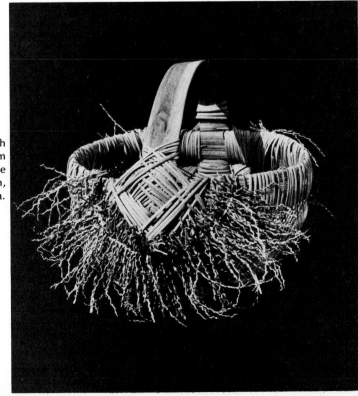

Flower basket. Japanese, early 20th century. Woven bamboo stained brown. Portions of the bamboo stem are exposed. 12 inches high, 9 inches wide. *Photographed at: The Gallery of Oriental Antiques, Palos Verdes Estates, California*

Detail of the basket, *left*, shows the continuous flow of the weavers from the handle to the basket body.

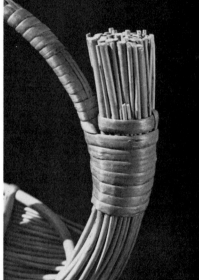

Various ideas for handles that you can use or alter, as needed, for your own baskets.

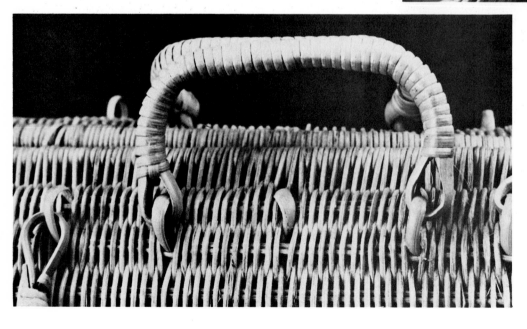

Study handle details of baskets from various cultures to observe the methods for attaching them, the materials used, and the hand-carved elements.

A woven reed basket with protruding reed ends on the bottom portion, illustrates a modern departure from a traditional method. 12½ inches high, 23-inch diameter. WICKER III. By Jude Silva. *Photo: George Lepp and Associates*

A birch twig basket has willows woven for the unusual built-up inside detailing that emphasizes the texture and design change. 26-inch diameter. SURFACING. By Elizabeth Schroeder. *Courtesy: artist*

A willow basket with a braided edge. By Sue Smith. *Courtesy: artist*

A rattan basket woven with repeats of dark brown and natural weavers. 9½ inches high, 8-inch diameter. By Kari Lonning. *Courtesy: artist*

A woven rattan lidded basket with willow bark inset. By Dodie Houghton. *Courtesy: artist*

A rattan sewing basket with "rope" handles made of braided cattail leaves. By Dodie Houghton. *Courtesy: artist*

Rattan and cane basket. Four-mm. rattan spokes were twined with 2-mm. rattan for the base and the beginning of the sides. Varying widths of split cane were used for the remainder of the sides. By working over different progressions of spokes, the abstract handle shaping was accomplished. 15 inches high, 9-inch diameter. By Margaret Henderson. *Photo: John Feche*

Round reed spokes were woven with split cane for this contemporary version of an Apache burden basket. The top ends of the spokes were wrapped with raffia and the raffia was braided for the hanging elements tipped with guinea hen feathers. 24 inches high, 14-inch diameter. By Mandy Arrington.

4 PLAITING

Is plaiting a weaving process? Or is weaving a plaiting process? Anthropologists have buffeted the question about for decades; their definitions are often bogged in wordiness with no definite conclusions. While experts continue to ponder a doubtful decision, it is more important to understand how weaving and plaiting are similar and how they differ.

The process of *weaving* as illustrated in chapter 3 involves *carrying the weft over and under one warp.* Weavers (weft) and spokes (warp) are defined and have specific functions. You always know which is which. A woven basket beginning can be easily observed by noting the directions of the spokes at the bottom.

A *plaited* basket *does not have a defined weft and warp.* All elements are worked in the *same under* and *over progression* as in weaving, *except* that in *plaiting* there is *no distinction made* between the *weavers* and the *spokes* as they are interwoven with one another. The plaited-basket beginning is not always obvious as in a woven base, although as the plaiting progresses beyond the base an uneven number of elements must be used as in weaving.

Plaited elements are usually flat, flexible and ribbonlike, but round elements can be used effectively. A plaited basket may or may not be sturdy enough to be rigid, depending on the materials used. For rigidity, the addition of a firm rim, base or uprights may be required. You will be able to observe this characteristic in the examples illustrated.

The usual beginning for a plaited basket

Plaited lidded basket of dyed and natural rivercane. (Chitimacha 1976.) 7¾ inches high. By Ada V. Thomas. *Courtesy: U.S. Department of the Interior, Indian Arts and Crafts Board*

is simply thus: The elements are woven under one and over one another to result in a square or rectangle for a basket where all the elements will be at right angles to one another. For a diagonal pattern basket, the elements are laid diagonally to one another and interwoven. Both beginnings are illustrated.

A form is shaped by bending or folding the unwoven portions of the elements and continuing to interweave them. Shaping may be accomplished by working over a fairly rigid form as shown in the following demonstrations. When one has sufficient expertise, the elements can be hand held and shaped as the work progresses. The shaping potential is so flexible that this traditional technique can be inventively adapted to contemporary statements and experimentation.

The demonstration beginning on page 60 shows dracaena draco leaves plaited in a right-angle pattern. The same procedures are used for any adaptable materials such as wood splints, reed, cane, yucca, flax, palm and cattail leaves, mulberry roots or straw. The natural orange stem ends of the dracaena draco leaves become both the decorative ending and the device that holds the elements in place. The drawing on page 62 illustrates the plaiting procedure beginning with a diagonal pattern and also using any of the materials mentioned.

You may have some difficulty, at first, keeping the woven portions together as you work outward. This may be overcome by temporarily

Soft, nested baskets of plaited palm in a South American marketplace have the often characteristic "corners" at the bottom with a cylindrical body.

Bamboo shrimp-catching basket, plaited, with overstitching for decoration. Shoulder rods reinforce the odd geometric shape. Free-ended spokes of the cover open and close to enable the fish to swim in, but prevent them from escaping. The Philippines, 1976. *Collection: Dona Meilach*

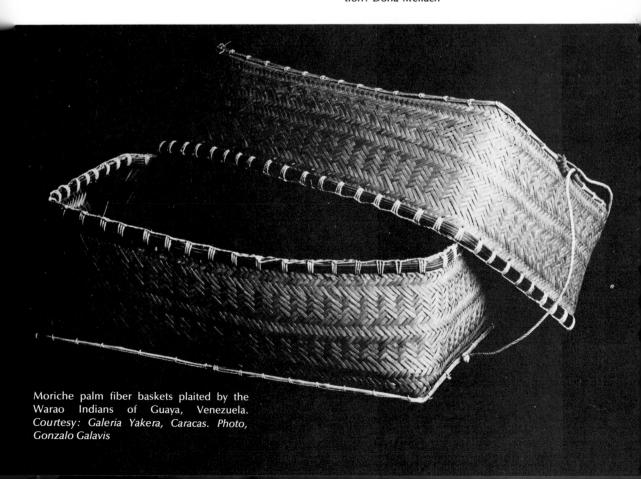

Moriche palm fiber baskets plaited by the Warao Indians of Guaya, Venezuela. *Courtesy: Galeria Yakera, Caracas. Photo, Gonzalo Galavis*

securing the elements over the form as shown on page 61. The elements should be quite damp as you work; if they are too dry, they may crack when they are bent for shaping.

The pattern potential within a plaited basket is infinite. Try alternating the weave progression and combining tabby, twill and other weave patterns described on page 32. Plaiting can be used as the base only and then combined with weaving or twining; then the plaited base elements actually change their role and become the warp (spokes) for woven or twined weft.

Adding color to the plaited basket will immediately create a new design dimension. Try alternating the elements in two different colors, then three colors. Using any two or three color schemes results in completely different designs when a right angle or a diagonal plait is used. Surface embellishments of the same color or of different colors are exciting to develop and will yield attractive results. We present examples and show how to develop three basic procedures for adding curls and twists.

Methods for ending the plaited basket are the same as those shown for weaving and twining though it should be reemphasized that for a rigid basket a sturdy rim is required if the plaiting is of soft materials.

A BASIC PLAITED BASKET

To plait a simple basket with natural materials, we suggest flat leaves such as the dracaena draco, prepared as shown in the weaving demonstration, page 32, but leave 8 of them whole. The leaves should be dampened. For a shaping form use a cardboard box covered with aluminum foil (to keep it dry) 8 × 8 × 12 inches high. Place 4 whole dracaena draco leaves horizontally across the bottom of the box and weave one leaf vertically through them, as shown. Note that the tips, which remain on for decoration, and the ends are alternated as each leaf is laid in place.

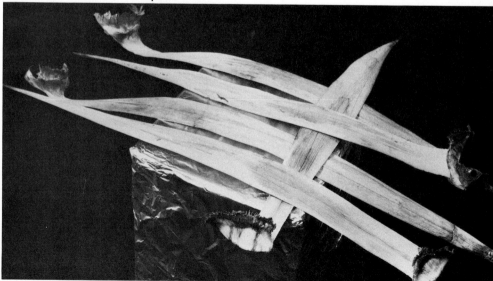

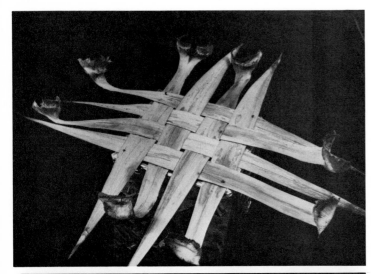

Weave three more whole leaves under and over the original set to form the plaited base, continuing to alternate the direction of the tip as each element is added. Place tacks at the corners to hold the plaited base in place.

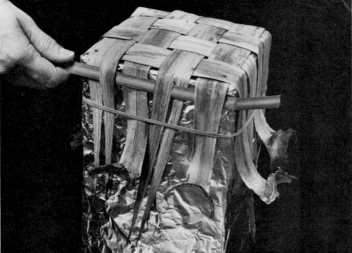

When the base is covered, leave one pointed leaf end whole and split all the other pointed tips. Fold all leaf ends down and secure them around the box with a rubber band or string. Begin to weave one narrow leaf at a time all around the box. When you work with short elements, such as leaves, use one leaf for each row and overlap the ends at a different place each time. When you use one long element such as cane, you can continue weaving around and around; overlap only where necessary as the weaver runs out.

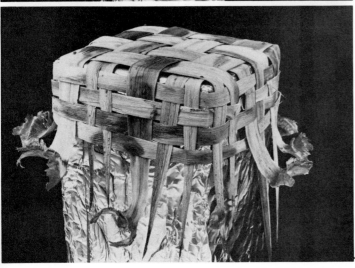

Continue row after row in the basic weaving pattern until you reach the height you want. This is the completed basket. The tacks will be removed and the basket carefully eased from the form. In this basket, the wide leaf ends form a natural border. In other types of materials the same finishes and rims shown for weaving and twining may be used.

Detail of the base of the basket, below, made of plaited philodendron sheaths laid on the base diagonally. The basket is 3½ inches square, 9 inches high. By Carolyn Thom.

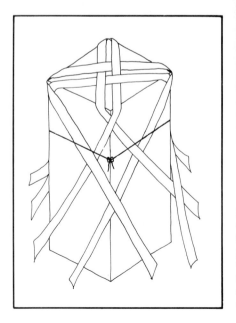

Begin the diagonal plaiting by placing 2 weavers from one corner to the opposite corner on top of the form. Then interweave these first pairs as shown. Continue to fill in with leaves woven in the tabby pattern and progressing from the center outward. Bend the weavers over the edges and secure them with a string until the pattern fills in all around.

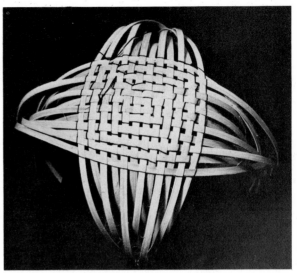

When a form is not practical, a string may be twined around each element to secure the plaiting and make the work easier to handle. Plait and twine in each row until the base is the size desired.

This procedure may result in a slightly rounded base that must be carefully shaped to keep it flat. Cut and remove the twined string after the base is completed. By Shereen LaPlantz. *Photos: David LaPlantz*

other method for holding the plaited elements as they are worked is to secure them th a scrap of fabric wrapped and tied und the base.

Plaiting may be combined with other techniques. A plaited bottom of cattail leaves is combined with raffia-twined sides. The plaited base elements become the spokes when the technique changes to twining. By Susan Marrant. *Photo: Joel Marrant*

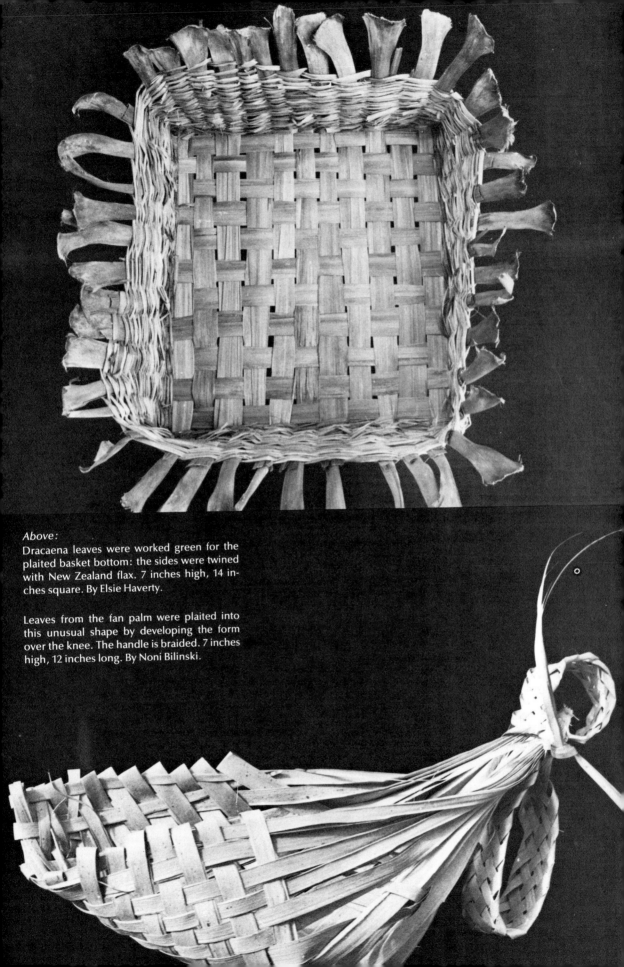

Above:

Dracaena leaves were worked green for the plaited basket bottom: the sides were twined with New Zealand flax. 7 inches high, 14 inches square. By Elsie Haverty.

Leaves from the fan palm were plaited into this unusual shape by developing the form over the knee. The handle is braided. 7 inches high, 12 inches long. By Noni Bilinski.

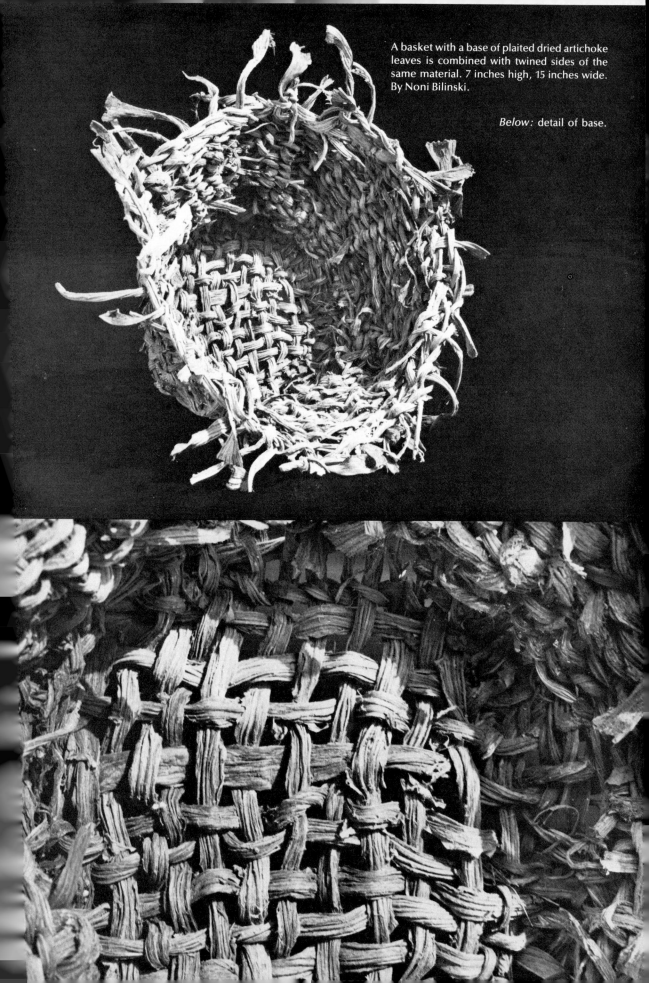

A basket with a base of plaited dried artichoke leaves is combined with twined sides of the same material. 7 inches high, 15 inches wide. By Noni Bilinski.

Below: detail of base.

ADDING COLOR TO PLAITED BASKETS

Color appears in plaited baskets in myriad and infinite patterning. A sampling of possible combinations follows. Observe the different plaited designs in the baskets you study and note whether two or more color elements are used and how they appear when they are plaited in a right-angle or a diagonal weave.

Color can be added by overlaying a narrow strip onto the wider plaiting elements as shown in the small basket below; then the color appears on the outer surface only and not on the inside.

Most often different colored elements are plaited to result in a checkerboard design, or a variation of it, depending on the under-over progression. If the color elements are toned on one side only, the basket will have two colors on the outside but remain only the natural color on the inside. Using three colors can result in an optical illusion of three dimensions on a two-dimensional surface.

A design can be planned to result in such geometrical shapes and variations of them as diamonds, squares and rectangles. Fragments of the shapes may be used or combinations of one shape within another.

Generally, an intricate pattern combination requires preplanning and/ or some experience with plaiting. It is a good idea to work out a pattern with strips of colored construction paper before you begin your basket.

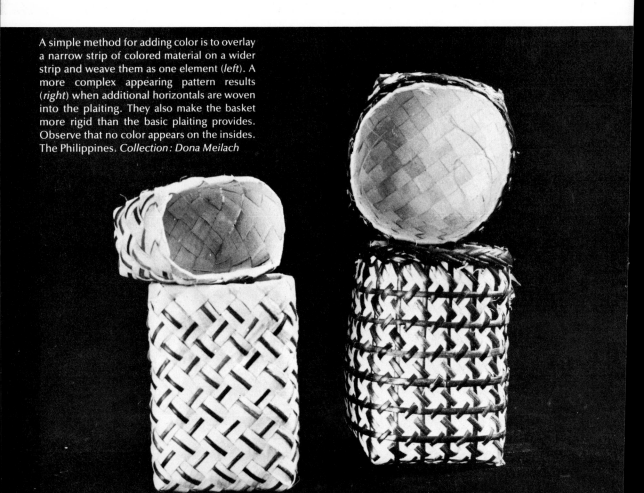

A simple method for adding color is to overlay a narrow strip of colored material on a wider strip and weave them as one element (*left*). A more complex appearing pattern results (*right*) when additional horizontals are woven into the plaiting. They also make the basket more rigid than the basic plaiting provides. Observe that no color appears on the insides. The Philippines. *Collection: Dona Meilach*

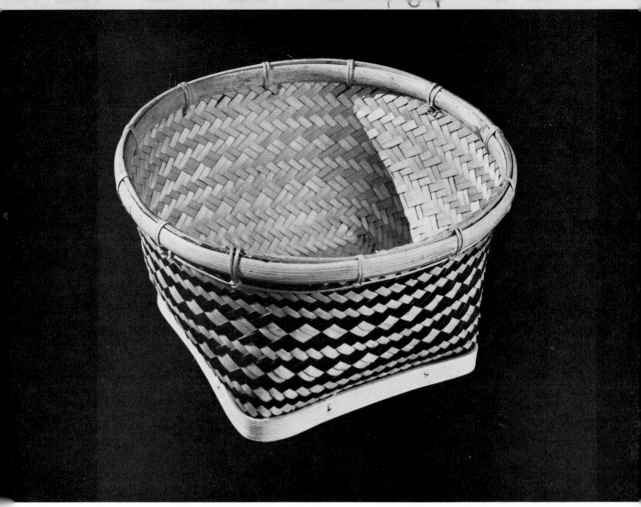

Plaited natural elements are combined with some that are colored on one side only for an appealing pattern contrast on the exterior. The rounded sides have been developed from a square base beginning. Rigidity is provided by the sandwich border and the splint around the bottom. *Collection: Mr. & Mrs. David W. Menagh, San Diego, California*

A Cherokee Indian basket has a distinctive pattern achieved by using vertical natural elements with horizontal colored elements. The intricate-appearing design results from weaving the horizontals over different numbers of spokes. It is quite simple to do and a variation is shown on the following page. Study the design progression carefully in any geometric pattern and you should be able to emulate it.

TWO-COLOR PLAITING

The following patterns have been developed with ½-inch strips of colored construction paper in two colors. After you see the results of these basic weaves, try others in two or three colors to develop your own patterns.

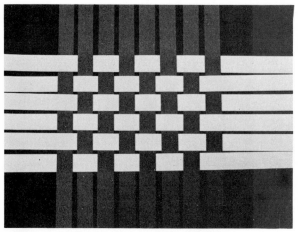

Tabby weave (under one, over one) with two color elements. The strips may be spaced slightly or pushed closely together. The materials used will help determine this placing.

This design, sometimes named "twilled twos," develops by working pairs of elements of unlike colors over other pairs of unlike color elements. The progression is over two, under two. It appears more complicated than it really is because of the use of two colors.

A diamond shape can be accomplished with two colors. Weave vertical rows with different colors of horizontal rows in stepped numbers. To yield the same color in the center in both directions, the beginning must have a horizontal and vertical of the same color: This is achieved by cutting the central colored horizontal row on each side to allow the crossover to show.

Another example of diamond design. Hopi sifter basket. Yucca leaves. *Collection: Mr. & Mrs. David W. Menagh. San Diego, California*

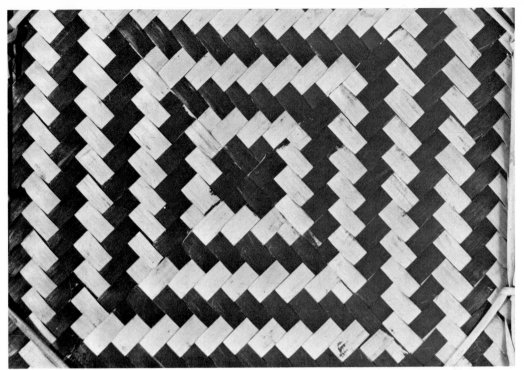

Detail of the base of a basket plaited in two colors with tabby weave.

By altering the progression of the weaves, you can develop any pattern you like. The right-angle weave changes from over one, under one, to double and triple progressions of one color over another. The shape is a contemporary adaptation of a traditional sifter basket. It is made of cattail leaves with split catalpa seed pods that provide the dark contrast color. By Sue Smith. *Courtesy: artist*

ADDING SURFACE CURLS AND TWISTS

Many cultures such as those of the American Indian, China, Japan, and the Philippines overlay a variety of curled and twisted strip designs to embellish the basket surface. Complex looking? Attractive? Rhythmic? Absolutely. Difficult? Not at all, once you try it and get the feel of it.

Shereen LaPlantz shares the curl and twist techniques inspired by the baskets of the Algonquian Indians of the Northeastern United States. Try the three simple curls and twists shown. Then alter the number of rows, the lengths and widths of the twists, add one over another and so forth for infinite variety.

Study the curl and twist embellishments on the baskets illustrated. Observe those in museums, in books and in basket shops for more ideas, then evolve your own designs of curls and twist rows on plaited or woven ready-made baskets as well as on those you create. Always work with long dampened strips of materials. For practice use a lightweight cardboard such as that cut from manila folders, but it probably will not bend the way a splint of wood will.

The Basic Curl

The basic curl uses two rows of horizontal weaving and three rows of verticals. For clarity, mark the weaver splint working end with an x. Number the horizontal rows 1 and 2. Letter the vertical rows a,b,c. The weaving splint would be very long so it can go as far as possible around the basket without piecing. To piece simply lay the new end under the old end.

Thread the weaver end x under a in row 1.

Curl back the weaver end x and thread it under b in row 2.

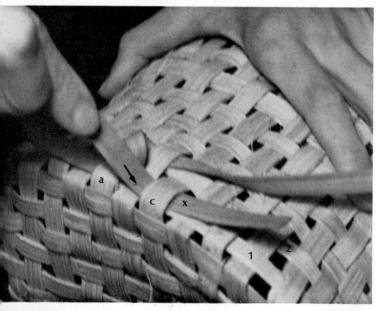

Pull it through only so far so that a short curl remains.

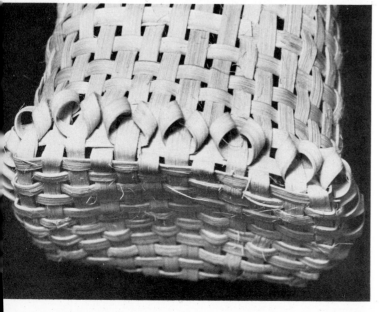

Thread end x under c in row 1 and pull through so a matching curl results.

Continue working around the basket using three verticals for each complete curl. The finished row will look like this.

The Elongated Curl

The elongated curl is also worked over three verticals (assign them the letters a,b,c). The one shown spans 4 horizontal weft rows; but it can be made longer or shorter. Shereen shows it going *over* the basic curl; it may be created by itself, over double curl rows and any other variation you choose. Use very long working splints dampened.

Thread x under a in row 1 under an existing basic curl, as shown.

Thread x under b in row 4 and pull only until it is the size curl you want.

Thread x under c in row 1. Continue the row using three vertical elements (a,b,c) for each curl, as shown.

The Tabby Twist Curl

Any row or series of rows can be worked with the tabby twist curl. Make it using the basic tabby (under one, over one) weave. It utilizes one horizontal row and three verticals. The thread end is woven under a vertical, then twisted around a finger before it is threaded under the next vertical. The twisted curl protrudes away from the basket and holds the shape in place.

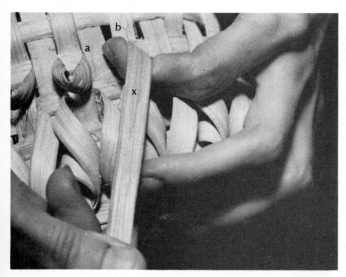

The tabby twist curl is worked by threading x under vertical a. Bring it out over b twisting it

Bring it back up, twist it again and thread it under c. c becomes the a of the next twist.

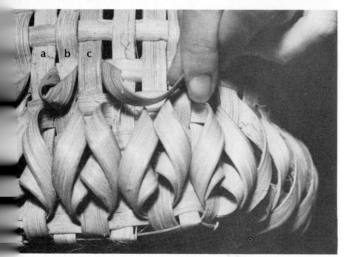

A finished twist. Continue working all around. Develop a working pattern and progression. Some people work better with the basket right side up; others upside down. See the following pages for a finished progression of the three basic curl twists that can be varied any way you like.

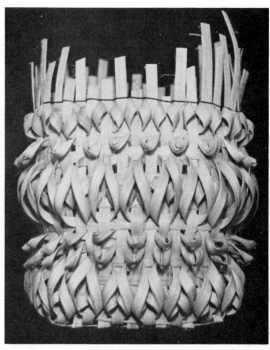

The twisted curls shown on the previous pages (*from bottom to top*): the basic curl, the elongated curl, two rows of tabby twist curl, a flat row, and a new row of basic curl.

Another row of elongated curls has been worked over the basic curl row, a single row of tabby twist curl and a single pattern of basic curl. Observe that Shereen uses a twined thread to hold vertical elements in place as she works. It will be removed when the rim is attached.

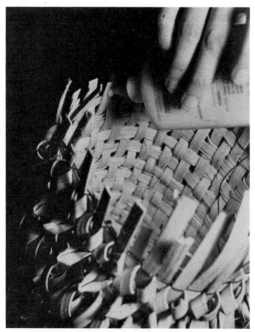

To finish the basket use the sandwich-rim technique. Depending on the materials the rims may be glued in place, as shown, or use any of the finishing techniques on pages 40–41.

A spring clip clothespin is a marvelous aid for holding basket elements in place as you work and as you glue vertical elements to rims.

The finished basket by Shereen LaPlantz. The verticals have been trimmed with a scissors, so they are even with the basket rim. *Demonstration: courtesy: Shereen LaPlantz Photos: David LaPlantz*

Three baskets by Shereen LaPlantz illustrate the variety of shapes one can make with simple plaiting and differently curled and twisted surface embellishments. *Photos: David LaPlantz*

Above:
Round and half-round reeds plaited. 7 inches high, 14-inch diameter.

Below left:
Ash splint basket unusually shaped. 12 inches high, 12 inches wide, 14 inches deep.

Below right:
Ash splint square basket. 4½ inches high, 4 inches square.

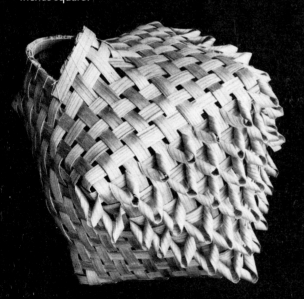

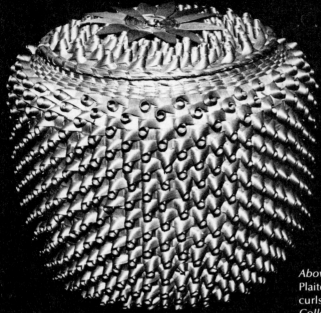

Above:
Plaited basket of the Winnebago Indians with curls around the surface and on the cover. *Collection: Field Museum of Natural History, Chicago Photo: Dee Menagh*

Below left:
Square palm-leaf basket with twists over the plaited elements. Mexico. 8 inches high, 8 inches square. *Private collection*

Below right:
The plaiting elements in this basket were twisted as the work progressed and resulted in negative areas at the pattern change rows. The Philippines. 8 inches long, 4 inches square. *Collection: Dona Meilach*

Plaited basket of ⅜-inch cane strips. China. 7 inches high, 15-inch diameter. *Collection: Mr. & Mrs. David W. Menagh, San Diego, California*

CANING

Caning is a form of plaiting often associated with furniture but the same procedures are used as in basketmaking.

A gourd used as a bottle is covered with cane. The body is worked in the chair-caning pattern; the neck is coiled and the base is twined. The hand-carved wood stopper is attached with a twisted cord. Thailand. *Photo and Collection: Edith Truesdale, Palo Alto, California.*

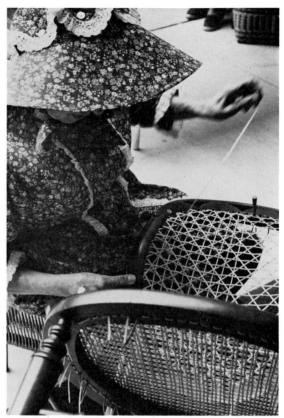

Caned chairs in different plaiting weaves by
H. & R. Causey.

Caned chair by H. Causey.

5 TWINING

Twining, like plaiting, also eludes exact definition by anthropologists and fiber authorities. It is usually categorized as a weaving technique with the characteristics that make it unlike weaving clearly explained. *Weaving* involves *working each weaver (weft) in turn, under and over the spokes* (warp). *Twining employs two weavers worked simultaneously;* they *cross over* one another between each spoke. *One weaver is taken behind* and *one in front* of the spoke and they enclose it. Some older basketry books refer to the technique as "pairing" because two elements are used. It has a characteristic twist and slant appearance that makes it easily identifiable from weaving when you are familiar with the two techniques.

Examples of twining used in fabric making as well as in basketmaking have been found in Peru and other South American sites dating back to about 2000 B.C. Twining has become extremely popular in the past few years as ancient fiber techniques have been explored. It may readily be combined with woven, braided, wrapped and knotted fiber works because of is versatility and structural potential.

The twining technique is easy to master; the form builds rapidly. When rigid spokes are used, the resulting structure is sturdy and rigid. Portions of the spokes may be exposed because the twined rows will remain where they are placed rather than slide up and down as would a woven row.

Both round and flat materials may be used for twining. The twining elements must be flexible and pliable so they can be manipulated in the crossover required between each spoke.

There are several procedures for beginning a twined basket. We show a

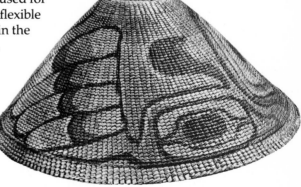

Painted hat, twined. Nootka Indians, Northwest Coast. Approx. 8 inches high, 15-inch diameter. *Photographed from the Collection, San Diego Museum of Man*

81

double overlapped base as one of the traditional methods. The same procedures used for a woven base are applicable to a twined structure.

Increasing the diameter of a twined basket is generally accomplished by adding spokes, by increasing the number of twists in the weavers between each spoke, by twining loosely or by switching to a larger diameter or wider weft materials. Woven and knotted portions can be combined with twined sections, which can also alter the diameter, shape and appearance of a basket.

Decreasing or reducing the form is done by twining over two or more spokes, dropping spokes, working the weft elements more tightly or using thinner diameter materials

Shaping may be accomplished by working the basket over a form as illustrated in chapter 2, page 26, or developed as you manipulate the form in your hands.

Finishing the twined basket can be accomplished by folding the spokes back into the work as in weaving, adding rims, wrapping, or utilizing the natural ending of the plant material if it lends itself to the treatment. It is almost always necessary that the last twining row be secured by some finishing method to prevent it from slipping up and causing the entire basket fabric to loosen.

Twined baskets from private collections and public markets should be examined as to how they were started, as to the the potential of their structures, the use of color and how the pieces are finished. We present ideas for all of these, but the vast range of possibilities is far greater than one chapter would allow.

Twined grass basket in vibrant dyed colors including blue, green, red and natural shades, with wrapped handles. Cajamarca, Peru. 23 inches high, 18 inches wide, 12 inches deep. *Collection: Dona Meilach*

Farmer's rain cape of twined rice straw and akita. Japan. *Courtesy and Collection: Mingei International (from Folk Arts of Japan), La Jolla, California*

TWINING PROCEDURES

A twined basket made with natural materials is generally started at the bottom center using any of a variety of methods shown on page 86. Even or uneven numbers of spokes may be used as opposed to weaving (chapter 3), which requires uneven numbers of spokes. However, the arrangement of spokes and the procedures for beginning the twined base are the same as those shown for a woven base. We also show the traditional overlapped double-base beginning and more ideas using flat and round materials that can be adapted to all techniques.

After the base is worked to the desired size, the spokes may be shaped upward by gently bending them and pulling the twining elements more tightly. They should be damp to prevent cracking. When the base is secured to a shaping block or other form (chapter 2), feel free to work with the form upside down or right side up, whichever is more comfortable for you. Creating interest in the sides of the twined basket can be accomplished by varying the materials used, by alternating twining with weaving, by expanding or decreasing the shape and by any of the scores of possible variations suggested by the examples that follow.

A variety of decorative and functional finishes are also shown. Generally, the same finishes shown for weaving (pages 40–41), including sandwiching, looping and braiding, are used on twined baskets also.

Basic Twining

Begin with a doubled length of twining material and cross over between each spoke, then enclose the spoke with *one element behind* and *one in front* of each spoke.

Compact Twining

When the second row is twisted in the *same direction* as the first row it has this appearance . . . and is called "compact twining."

Counter Twining

When the twist is *reversed* on the second row, this appearance results and is called "counter twining." Rows of compact twining may be interspersed with rows of counter twining for design details.

Changing Progressions

Design changes can be achieved by altering the progression of the twining over varying numbers of spokes in different rows. Twining over two spokes in the top rows creates a different pattern than twining over individual spokes as in the bottom row. When two different colored or textured weavers are used for several rows a vertical striping occurs.

Adding New Lengths

Adding twined lengths of some materials requires laying the new length (a) behind one spoke and cutting the old end (b) off so it is hidden behind a different spoke. When both twining elements shorten simultaneously do not put both new ends behind the same spoke; rather stagger them. If ends of both elements are placed behind the same set of spokes throughout, the pattern will be off somewhat, and a weak spot may occur in the basket.

The addition has this appearance from the other side. The new lengths will be lost in the work as it progresses. Also see page 87 for another way to add new elements.

Twining Flat Material

When flat elements are used for twining they should be twisted and neatly laid around the spokes.

BASES AND HOW TO BEGIN THEM

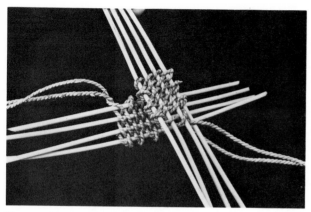

The overlapping double base consists of two sets of twined spokes placed at right angles.

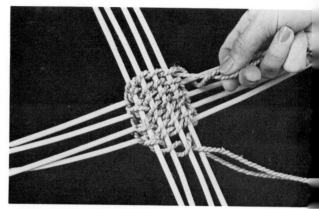

The spokes are spread and the twining proceeds using the long doubled elements from one base. The ends from the second base will be tucked in between the bases.

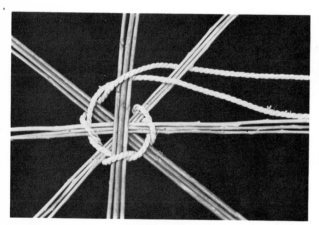

Soaked flexible tree branches are laid out in groups of three and twined with sea grass. Loop the doubled sea grass element over one branch group and begin to twine around each group.

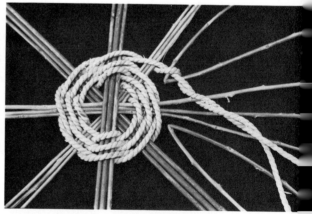

As the twining circumference increases, the groups are spread and each branch is twined individually. Additional spokes are added by inserting bent branches at the points of increase and each side of the bend is twined in individually. The basket shape can be determined by the arrangement of additional spokes. If two increases are added on opposite sides, the basket will become an oval. Four increases spaced in opposite "corners" will yield a symmetrical square or round shape.

Flat spokes may be interwoven to form a square beginning, then twined. Add single spokes with flat materials by tapering the ends and poking them into the work. As the twining continues incorporate the additions. Add new twining elements between existing spokes. Do not add them at corners or between additions as these are the weak points of the structure.

Another type base evolves when two groups of spokes are laid at right angles to each other, then groups are twined to hold them together. The first row of twining over 4 spokes requires a double twist at each corner for two rows, then basic twining over each spoke individually. To achieve a round shape without adding spokes with this beginning, bend the spokes outward. As the circumference increases single spokes can be added as in the preceding photo. Add a new doubled element back a few spokes and allow the old ends to stagger so they are lost within the twining without creating a bump (see photo on page 85).

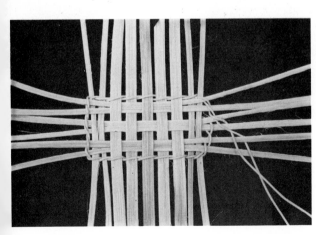

An oval or rectangular shape emerges when unequal numbers of spokes are interwoven in opposite directions, as shown. Observe that some elements have been split to yield the desired number of spokes. The corners may be spread so the desired shape is accentuated. Extra spokes may be added at the corners as needed.

A BASIC TWINED BASKET

Maxine Kirmeyer demonstrates the procedures for making a basic twined basket with prepared coconut palm cord, jute, sea grass and leaves. (You can use any similar commercially prepared flexible round material such as sea grass, sisal or jute.)

Cut 6 spokes each 30 inches long of coconut palm cord. Wrap tape around the spoke ends to prevent unraveling, if necessary. Lay 3 spokes crosswise over 3 other spokes and begin to twine with 5-ply jute for the beginning only. Jute is thinner than the coconut palm and more manageable for starting the base.

Spread the spokes out evenly to make a circle.

With the jute, continue to twine over each spoke for 3 rows.

Secure the loose jute ends under the twining rows with a crochet hook . . .

. . . and snip them off.

Change your twining cord to the coconut palm for a different texture and to increase the basket circumference. Twine for 2 rows.

It will have this appearance when the spokes are properly spaced and twined. The circumference should be slightly larger than the coffee can that will be used for the shaping form.

Center the coffee can on the base, bend the spokes up and begin to twine around the sides of the form working upward. (You can use any form you like such as a roll of paper towel, a jar or a box. It need not be a coffee can.)

Below left:

The twining progresses as it is pulled tightly to the shape of the form.

Below right:

The form may be removed once the basic shape is established, as shown. Or it may be left in until the last row, depending on the side treatment and shaping desired.

Dampened leaves are added at this point for one row followed by 3 rows of commercially prepared sea grass. These provide variety and textural interest.

Ending the basket. You have two choices. You may cut the ends about 1 inch above the basket and let the ends spread naturally.

Below left:

Or the other way to end the basket is to bend each spoke and tuck it into the last twining rows.

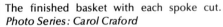

The finished basket with each spoke cut. *Photo Series: Carol Craford*

Twisted, commercially prepared sea grass twined over palm spokes. 12 inches high, 8-inch-square base. By Maxine Kirmeyer. *Photo: Carol Craford*

Colored raffia twined over commercially available paper "rope" with leafed olive branches wrapped into the top spoke endings. 9½ inches high, 12-inch diameter. By Shirley Sestric-Friedlander.

Dracaena leaf spokes with twined areas of New Zealand flax and honeysuckle vines (2 views). 15 inches high, 12-inch diameter. By Roberta Foster.

Spokes of fan palm leaves have been twined
with sweet grass and raffia and combined with
rows of woven fan palm. 14 inches high, 6-
inch-square base. By Marge Bardacke.
Courtesy: artist

Raffia twined over twisted commercially prepared sea grass. The square shape begins with the overlapped double base and is worked over a milk carton. 15 inches high, 6 inches square. By Chris Olofson.

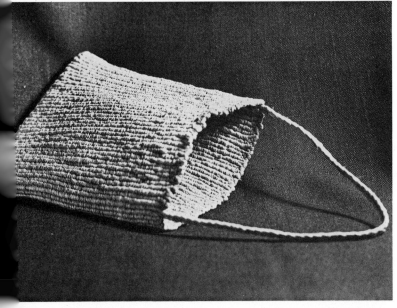

Raffia twined over sea grass for a storage bag. 8½ inches long, 6¾ inches wide. By Nancy Waerhouse. *Photo: Sally Davidson*

Raffia twined over sea grass. 15 inches long, 8 inches wide. By Chris Olofson.

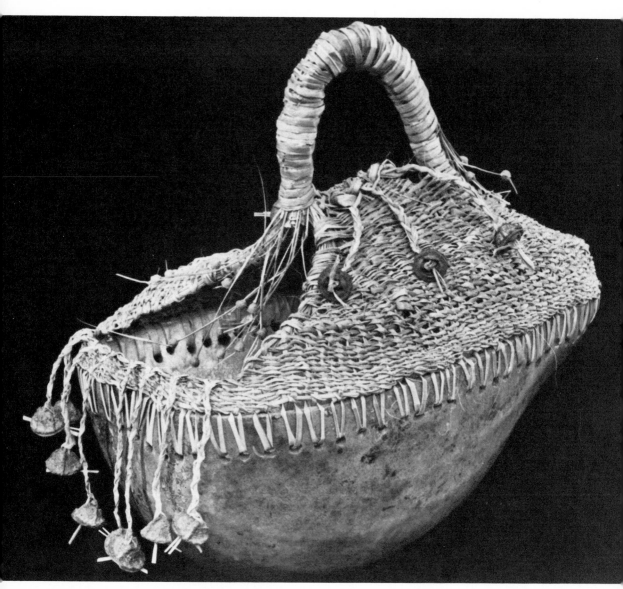

Guatemalan gourd cut and drilled, then twined with New Zealand flax lashed to the base. Eucalyptus seed pods have been added for decorative endings. 13 inches high, 16 inches wide. By Misti Washington. *Collection: David Anderson, Del Mar, California*

A variety of different shaped baskets twined with twisted palm leaves and lily leaves over flat palm leaf spokes. The bases are plaited and the elements become the spokes for the twining used on the sides only. Each basket has a different ending treatment. Average size: 5 inches high, 6-inch diameter or square base. By Melda D. Montgomery. *Courtesy: artist*

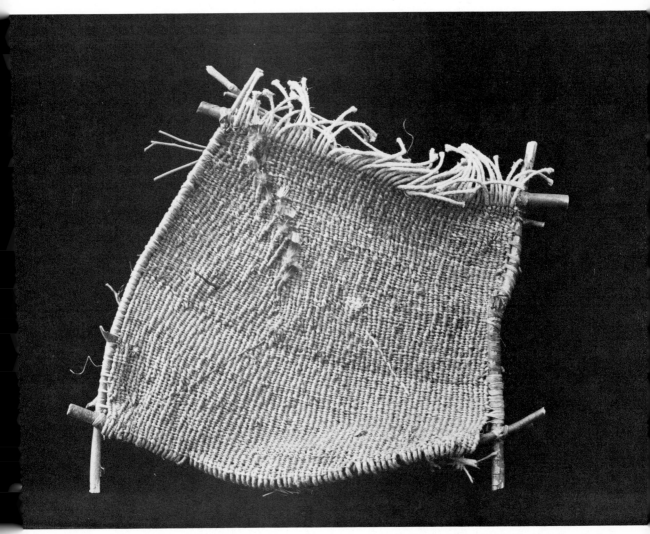

Opposite: top
Palm fronds, coconut palm cord, and euca-lyptus bark were worked over a 6-inch block of wood. Eucalyptus pod "beads" were drilled and strung with raffia. 7 inches high, 9 inches square. By Maxine Kirmeyer. *Photo: Carol Craford*

Bottom:
Eucalyptus bark forms a panel within the twin-ing and spokes of straw rope and coconut palm cord. The form was worked over a gasoline can. When the wet bark and other materials were removed from the form, they dried to a slightly different and delightful shape. 11 inches high, 13-inch diameter. By Maxine Kirmeyer. *Photo: Carol Craford*

A contemporary interpretation of an Indian ceremonial platter. The outer frame made of branches has been warped with polished jute, then twined with red and gray raffia. Tiny feathers of turquoise, purple and off-white have been worked into the twining. The re-verse side has additional pieces of roots, twigs, feathers and strawberry plants, which carry out the Indian symbolism. The basically flat shape is 17 inches × 14 inches. By Shirley Sestric-Friedlander.

Cattail leaves were twined over a base made of the entire palm frond. The detail, below, shows the base and how it was begun. When the whole frond is used, it tends to result in a free-form basket shape. Approx. 15 inches high, 18 inches wide. By Janet Martini.

Cattail leaves twined over oak splints. The base is plaited and some of the wide splints are incorporated into the basket sides. Observe the pattern change created by alternating the twining pattern over different groupings of spokes. Approx. 18 inches high, 15 inches square. By Janet Martini.

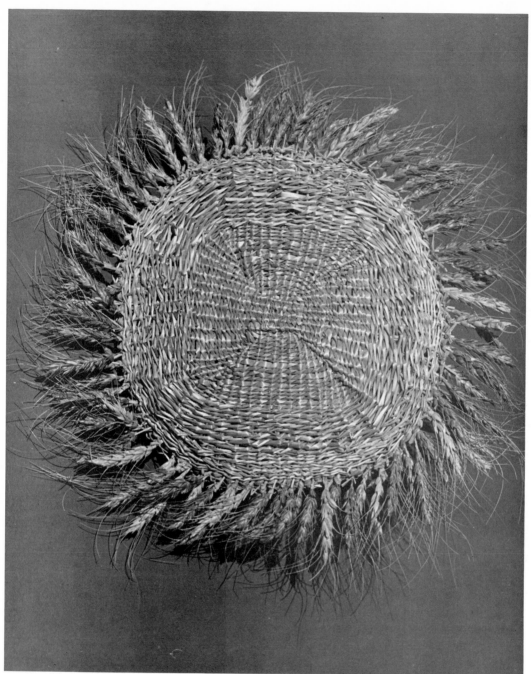

Wheat stalks with some of the heads remaining were used for twining and for decoration. Reed spokes are worked into a woven finish at the basket top. Approx. 14-inch diameter. By Sue Smith. Base detail (*above*) shows the overlapping double beginning. Basket (*below*). *Courtesy: artist*

A hanging basket with extended twig details was inspired by a traditional Appalachian basket. New Zealand flax was twined over apricot twigs. 21 inches high, 12 inches wide. By Sue Kamin.

A large melon-shape basket made of cattail leaves twined over lemon twig spokes. 20 inches high, with handle, 20-inch diameter. By Louise Meeks.

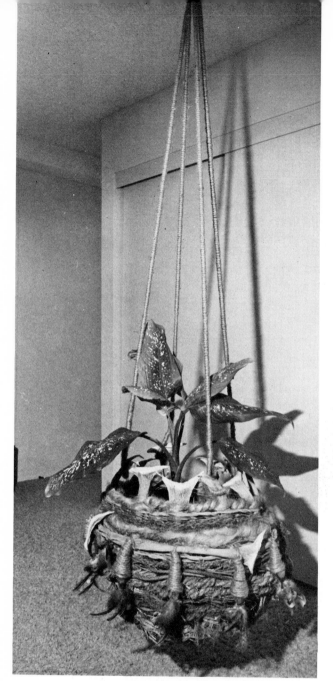

A large hanging basket is composed of a variety of natural materials including yucca leaves, cattail leaves, star pine cones, feathers. The basket portion is 21 inches high, 21-inch diameter. By Linda Zaiser.

Above right:

The fan form is made of reed spokes. The twining is waxed linen and yarn with pheasant feathers at the spoke tips. Eucalyptus seed pod embellishments are at the center and on the handle. 12-inch diameter. By Jean Freeland. *Courtesy: artist*

Right:

Shapes can be made separately of many techniques and assembled for a sculptural presentation. Sea grass spokes were twined with raffia: with other portions coiled, knotted, woven and wrapped. By Dawn Rose Schiro. *Photo: Leep and Associates*

Twined day lily leaves over willow branch spokes. Day lily leaves, gathered after the first frost, yield lovely natural shades of oranges, yellows, rusts and browns. By Sue Smith. *Courtesy: artist*

Palm frond spokes with twined sea grass and goat hair yarn. Separating the spokes and twining them in different progressions results in the negative shape. See layout. 18 inches high. By Susan Aaron-Taylor. *Courtesy: artist*

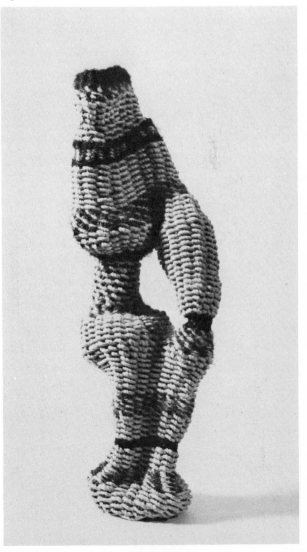

Twined sea grass with driftwood. Side and top views. Approx. 15 inches high. By Jacqueline Wry.

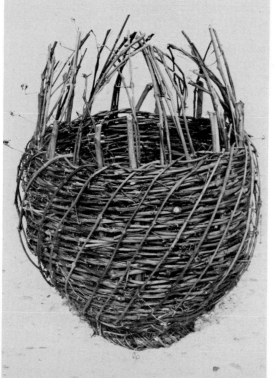

Twined grapevine basket with branches added on the outside for the linear detail. Approx. 15 inches high. By Dorothy Gill Barnes. *Courtesy: artist*

Assembled shapes created from New Zealand flax twined over date palm seed fronds. 19 inches high, 8½ inches wide. By Irene Pfeiffer.

Raffia twined over reed with added feathers and shells. The lashed legs are palm stems. Approx. 15 inches high, 8-inch diameter. By Mary Ann Taggart. *Photo: Buchner and Young.*

Top:

African headdress basket. Natural raffia twined around twisted cattail leaves. The piece was worked wet and flat. When it was partially dried, it was folded and enclosed at the top. The sides remain open to form a container. 15 inches high, 20 inches wide. By Laurie Dill.

Center and bottom:

Inspiration for minimally twined pieces can be gleaned from a variety of sources such as a Peruvian rolled-up carrying sheaf (*above*) or the primitive hut exhibited in a diorama (*right*).

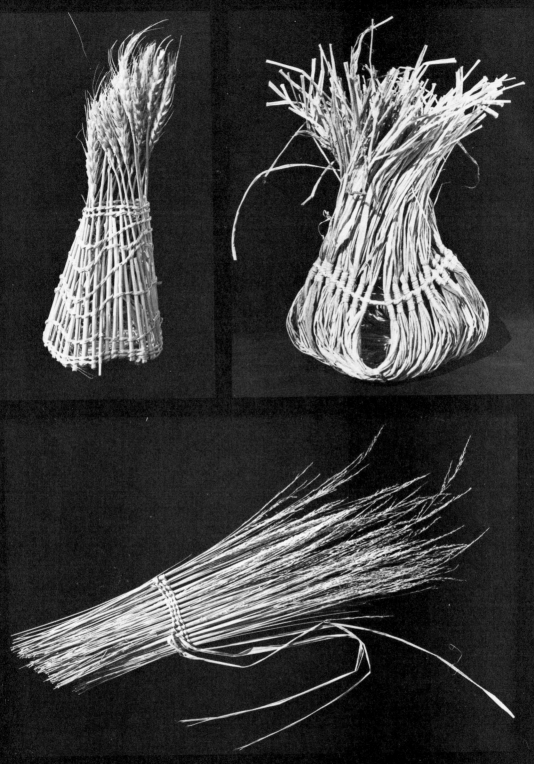

Top left:
Wheat stalks twined with raffia. 12 inches high, 5-inch bottom diameter. By Millie Crowell.

Top right:
Natural reed twined with raffia. 10 inches high, 18-inch diameter. By Laurie Dill.

Bottom:
Minimal twining with raffia over graduated lengths of grasses. 15 inches long, 7 inches wide. By Dee Menagh.

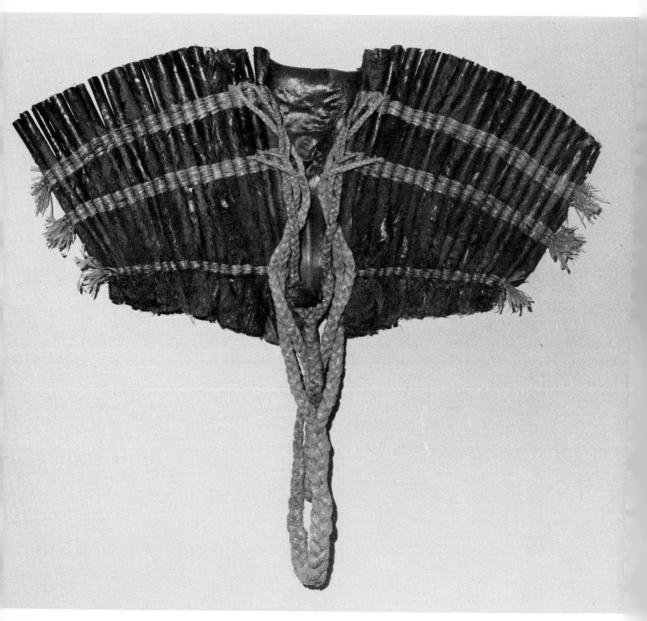

Palm bark rolled into thin cylinders laid together and twined with raffia. Braided raffia for the center over a palm element. Approx. 24 inches high plus hanging portion. 36 inches wide. By B. J. Adams. *Photo: Clark Adams*

Long Florida pine needles are twined and supported with wrapped reeds. A coiled base is
set in and stitched to secure it. 14 inches high,
6-inch base spreading to an 18-inch-top
diameter. By Jeannie Vaughn MacDougall.
Courtesy: artist

6 COILING

Coiling is a traditional basketmaking procedure often categorized as a "sewing" technique. It has been used for centuries by countless numbers of cultures. The "core" of the basket is a relatively flexible material that is usually worked in a coil or spiral-like shape. Another material is wrapped around the core, then sewn to adjacent coils to hold the elements together.

A basket *core* may be a twig, root, flexible branch such as a length of willow or reed. It may also be composed of bunched materials: grasses, leaves, straw, cornhusks, pine needles, jute, sisal and other ropelike fibers.

The *wrapping* can be grasses, flexible splints, raffia, plied ropes and yarns or any flexible material that can be wrapped and pulled through and/or around the adjacent coils. Stiffer materials, reed and branches, for example, may be easily manipulated by sharpening the tips as the wrap is worked through the coils; more flexible materials will require the use of a needle or other sharp sewing device.

Any materials that tend to crack as they are worked, either the core or the wrap, must be dampened. Raffia, jute and similar very flexible materials are worked dry.

The coil, usually begun from the bottom, can be developed into a round, oval, square or rectangular base. The side shape can, but does not necessarily have to, follow the shape of the base. For example, a cylindrical form can be made over a square base, or a free-form piece can evolve from a round base. Analysis of the

Coiled pattern basket. Pomo Indian. *Photographed from the Collection: San Diego Museum of Man*

113

examples that follow will underscore the potential variety of the technique for a modern application of traditional coiling.

Historical examples of coiled baskets preserved in collections illustrate a magnificent craftsmanship and orderly progression of the coils in a geometric arrangement with simple or intricate patterning. The materials were indigenous to the environments of the people who created them. The baskets were utilitarian and usually steeped in tradition and ritual.

Contemporary coiled baskets still rely on impeccable craftsmanship, but the freedom of materials used and the shapes that evolve may be nontraditional. They can be conceived and dramatically designed as an artistic expressive statement. Today's basket artist does not have to adhere to symbology, tradition, location of materials, or to be concerned with function. And therein lies his ability to explore the potential of the technique with a wide choice of materials.

Observe, experiment with, practice and master the basic coiling procedure, then bend these "rules" to play your own game and to make your own statements. The following stitches employed in coiling will be your basic technique vocabulary: Lazy Stitch, Figure 8 Stitch, the Split Stitch, and the Lace Stitch. After you learn the basic stitches observe detailing on baskets from various cultures to analyze the many variations. For example, a single Lazy Stitch may alternate and span two coils, then one coil, for a surface pattern. Imbrication, another decorative technique, is shown on page 135.

Intricate and symmetrical basket designs, such as those presented in American Indian baskets, require careful preplanning. It is wise to sketch the pattern on paper before beginning, then divide the design into sections, perhaps quadrants, depending on the basket shape and design. Each section must be carefully worked onto the coiling to achieve the desired effect.

Natural materials used for coiling may be selected for the tones or colors they yield. Bright colors, not found in nature, can be added by dyeing the materials. Beads, feathers, shells, seed pods, wrapping and other embellishments can be creatively added.

Oval patterned coiled basket. Pomo Indian.
Photographed from the Collection: San Diego Museum of Man

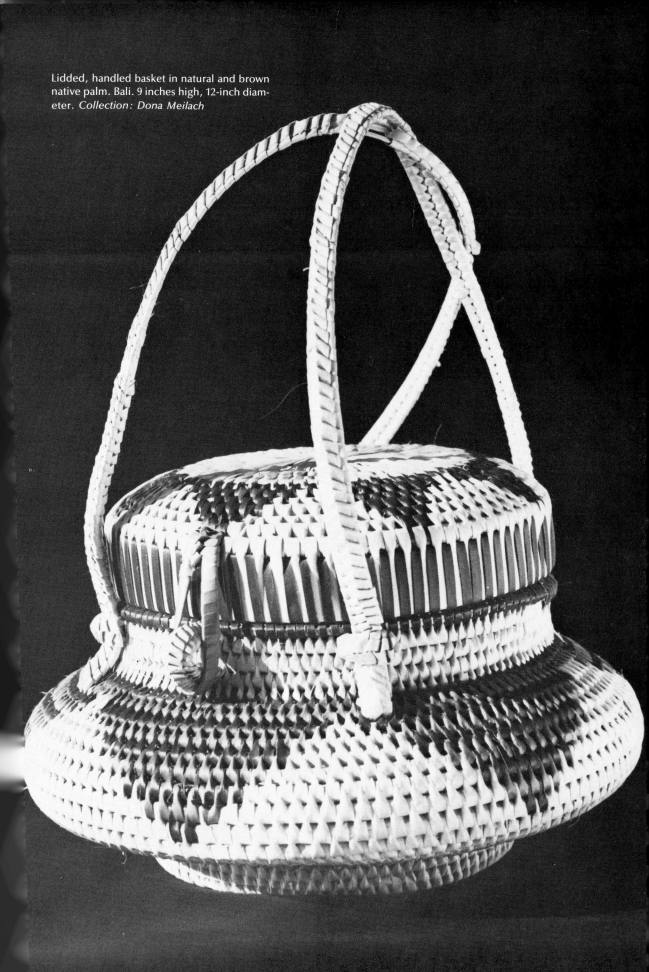

Lidded, handled basket in natural and brown
native palm. Bali. 9 inches high, 12-inch diameter. *Collection: Dona Meilach*

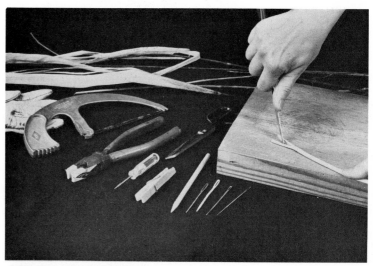

COILING PROCEDURES
Materials and tools for coiling with natural materials are (*counterclockwise*) branches and leaves, gloves, saw, pliers with masking tape over the tips, awl, scissors, spring clip clothespin, pointed dowel (can be pointed in a pencil sharpener), plastic and metal needles, cutting board, knife. A reed is split with the knife on the cutting board.

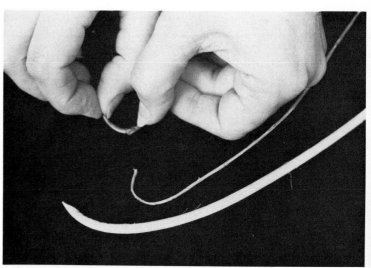

The end of a branch to be used for the basket core must be gently bent. Work the branch end between your fingers back and forth several times to break down the fibers and make it pliable . . . but be careful not to crack it.

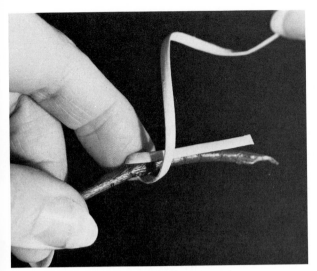

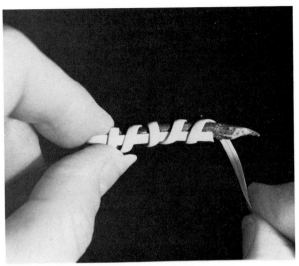

Start a basket using a branch for the core and split cane for the wrapping material. Taper the branch end. To begin wrapping, lay the end of the cane parallel with the branch and bring the cane around the branch, and over.

Wrap the end tightly along the branch. The working tip of the cane wrapping should be cut to a point. A needle is not used with a stiff material.

Bend the branch and pull the wrapping so the branch end makes a loop. Attach the top of the tip to the core as shown leaving a hole at the center. The hole should be small, but large enough to accommodate additional lengths of cane being pulled through it *only for the first coil.*

Continue to bend the core and wrap until one full coil is made. As you bend the core, and the second coil begins, the cane tip is inserted under every other wrapping on the preceding coil. Continue to work in any pattern buildups and shaping desired following the drawings of coiling methods that follow.

Beginning the Coil

The following series shows the coiling technique as it is adaptable to a variety of materials. These are general procedures. You may have to thread the wrap through a needle when the materials are very flexible such as grasses, raffia, jute, split leaves and so forth. For stiff wrapping materials such as split cane or split reed, taper the end to a point so you can slip it between the coils.

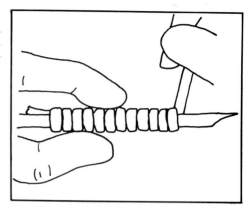

Taper the core material. Lay the wrap material parallel with the core and about 2 inches from the tapered end. Overlap the first wind to secure it. Wrap to about ½-inch from the tapered end.

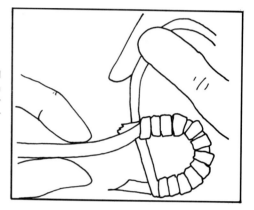

Bend the tapered end of the core and wind the wrapping around the bent section to form and secure it in a tight circle, leaving only enough space in the center to bring your needle through.

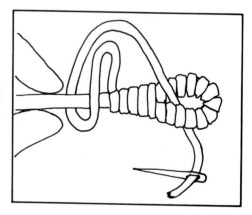

Continue to wrap until the tapered core end is secure. Bring the needle through the center and pull the wrap tightly. (For illustration only, the center hole is shown enlarged.)

Wrap the core and bring the needle through the center again, shaping the coil into a circle as you work. The number of wraps can vary depending on the material you use. It can be twice, three times or more. Tie an identifying string at the beginning of this row. This will help you form the basket neatly and evenly. Whenever you begin to shape, add a color, change stitches, and end the basket, it should be done in line with this "point of movement."

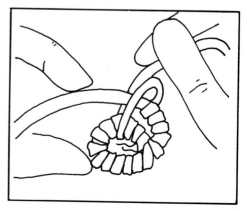

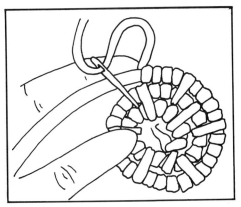

LAZY STITCH

The Lazy Stitch is made by bringing the wrap over two coils to form a radiating pattern on the basket surface. It is made by wrapping the top coil the established number of times and bringing the wrap over the preceding coil. NOTE: The needle is brought back to the center ONLY for the initial coil; in all subsequent rows it is placed over only the adjacent coil . . . you DO NOT go back to the center again.

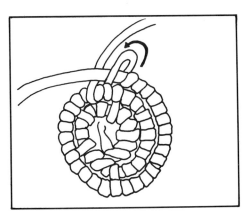

FIGURE 8

The Figure 8 Stitch is carried between the coils rather than spanning two coils as in the Lazy Stitch. It does not create the radiating pattern. Carry the wrap over the top core, behind the bottom adjacent core, under it, in front of and behind the top core. It does not matter whether you work from back to front, as shown, or from front to back.

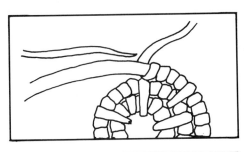

ADDING NEW WRAPPING LENGTHS

When your wrapping material shortens, new lengths are added in the following manner so they do not create a bulge or a knot on the basket.

Lay one end of the new length along the core in the direction you are wrapping.

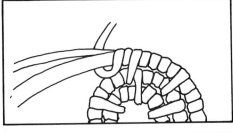

Secure this end beneath the short end of the old wrap for 2 or 3 winds.

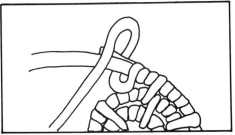

Lay the end of the old wrap on the core; pick up the new wrap and begin to wind it securing the end of the old beneath. Wrap tightly and continue to work with the new length.

LACE STITCH

The Lace Stitch provides a decorative detailing that may be worked over the Lazy Stitch or the Figure 8 Stitch. It is used to create a space between coils and a lacy appearance. The stitch may be made using one or more wraps. The greater number of wraps used, the larger the resulting space between the coils.

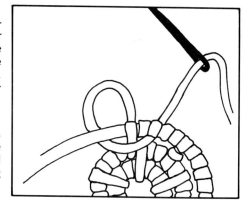

With the stitch over or between the two coils, bring the wrapping around and over the strand (from left to right and behind it) and continue to work by wrapping and attaching in the basic stitch pattern you are using.

For a greater space between the coils, and a more open appearance, take two or more winds around each stitch.

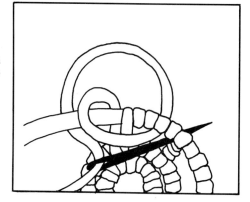

SHAPING

The basket shape is determined by how one coil is placed onto another. When you make the bottom flat, the coils are laid next to one another. As the basket sides are worked upward, simply place a coil onto the adjacent coil in the direction you want the side to take. For a straight side, the shaping coil would be placed directly on top of the last bottom coil. For a gradual curve, the shaping coil would be placed at about a 45 ° angle to the bottom coil. Always begin to shape upward at a point in line with your "point-of-movement" identifying tie.

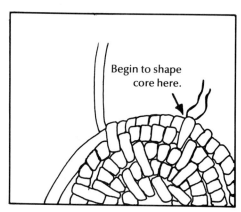

Begin to shape core here.

FINISHING

The end of the core can be tapered and tightly wrapped in using a needle wrap. The very tip of the end should line up with the point of movement. Depending on the thickness of the core, taper it to a point about one or more inches from the end. Finish wrapping and insert the needle back under the final wrappings and pull through. Use a pliers, if necessary.

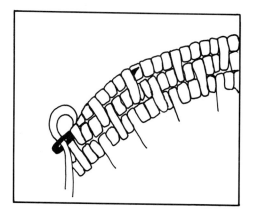

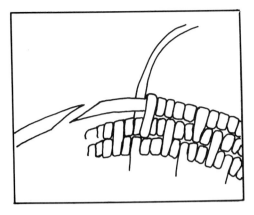

ADDING CORE

When your core material shortens, add a new length by tapering the ends of each and laying them next to one another and wrap over them.

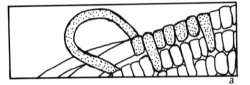

ADDING COLOR

A new color may be added in the same way a new length of wrapping is added (page 119). Colors may be carried along the cores and picked up as needed for patterning.

a. When the new color is used as the wrapping it appears as a stitch on the adjacent coil and creates a pattern. The original color is carried beneath.

b. When you do *not* want the new color to appear on the adjacent coil (for making hard-edge diamonds and squares, for example), wrap with the new color, but carry the original beneath it; then use the original color to secure the stitch to the coil below.

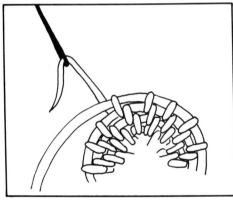

EXPOSED CORE

Many baskets are made so that the wrapping material is spaced and allows the core material to show. Exposed core baskets progress more quickly than those where every inch of core is wrapped. Often the contrast between the natural color of the core and the wrapping is beautiful and desirable. Any stitches illustrated may be used. The wrapping must be done neatly and the ends carefully laid in so they will not show and intrude upon the pattern.

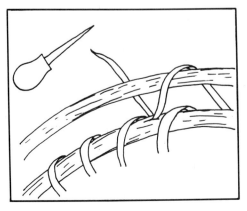

USING AN AWL

When a core of bunched grass material is used, it is often desirable to bring your stitch through the top of the preceding coil rather than all the way around it. Then it is necessary to pierce a hole in the top of the coil with the point of an awl or other sharp-pointed instrument so that you create a space through which the wrapping material can be threaded.

Coiled eucalyptus branches. 24 inches high, 6½-inch diameter. By Shirley Sestric-Friedlander.

Right:
Unspun sisal over a reed core with pieces of reed pushed through the soft surface. Basket top (*detail below*), 11 inches high, 8-inch diameter. By Shirley Sestric-Friedlander.

Left:
CLIMB FOUR. Natural raffia, tar treated and aged sisal over a sisal core. The form was inspired by a mountain and designed to hold gifts from the Sierra Nevada. 15 inches high, 11-inch rectangular base. Detail of the two parts below. By Dawn Nielsen. *Courtesy: artist*

Above:
Raffia over a reed core and (*below*) raffia over
a sea grass core. Both are freely shaped with
assembled parts. Duck feathers and black lin-
en are added in the basket below. By Brynn
Jensen. *Courtesy: artist*

Blue mohair over a reed core with down
feathers added at the top. By Brynn Jensen.
Courtesy: artist

Natural raffia over a fiber hemp core with
exposed chestnut horsehair. 5 inches high, 5
inches wide. By Karen McCarthy. *Courtesy:
artist*

Brown coconut fiber core coiled and stitched with brown cotton string. 9 inches high, 13-inch diameter. By Ann Dunn. Detail below.

Core of palm tree fiber with willow overlays coiled with brown string. Some stitching. 8½ inches high, 6-inch diameter. By Shirley Sestric-Friedlander. Detail below.

Date palm flower stems coiled and allowed to protrude from the surface. They are wrapped with natural color raffia. Two views. 7½ inches high, 10-inch diameter. By Jacqueline Sherman.

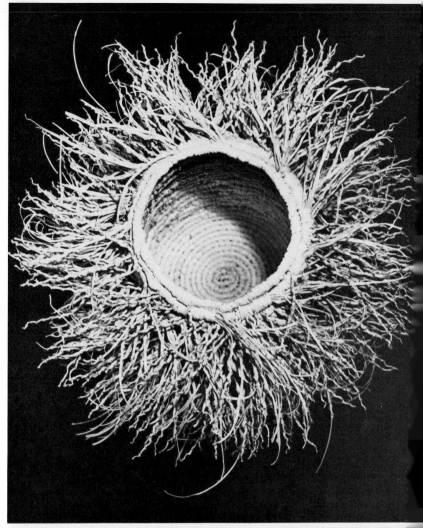

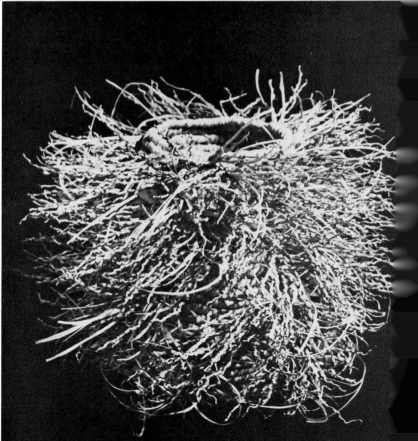

Honeysuckle vines in varying thicknesses were used for both core and wrapping. 18 inches high, 10-inch diameter. By Peat Louisa O'Neal. *Photo: Susan Seligman*

Plaque. Yucca leaves wrapped over a grass core. Hopi Pueblo Indians. 1964. Indian baskets are noted for their color and pattern. They provide constant inspiration for contemporary baskets such as those at right. 14½-inch diameter. By Grace Vance. *Courtesy: U.S. Department of the Interior, Indian Arts and Crafts Board*

Right:
Colored raffia wrapped over reed core materials are used for the elegantly shaped and colored baskets. By Jude Silva. *Photos: Stephen E. Stuntz*

Detail and basket made of raffia over reed with an added detail of back-stitched sisal between the coils. 8 inches high, 10-inch diameter. By Chris Olofson.

HOW TO BACKSTITCH

Any kind of decorative material may be added to a finished basket. The backstitch, associated with embroidery, adapts to basketry embellishment. Place the stitch over the vertical wrapping and add this horizontal detail.

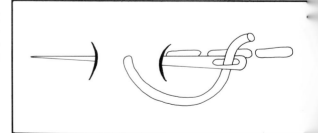

Raffia over pine needles with palm leaves extending for the exterior detail, called "Imbrication," on 3 of the rows. Imbrication, also called Klikitat, is an exterior addition accomplished as the coiling progresses (*see below*). By Annabel Bergstrom Woodsmall.

IMBRICATION

Imbrication is accomplished by laying a material on the surface of the core and doubling it back before stitching it to the core with the wrapping. The Imbrication design can be combined with rows designed in other stitches and patterns.

Coil 1. Lay the surface material along a coil and secure it with the wrappings. Continue to develop the coils but fold the surface material so it protrudes before securing it with the next stitch. Repeat this "fold and secure" process with each stitch taken. It is easiest to do with the Lazy Stitch.

As you progress, attach the coils together without disturbing the raised addition. You may pass the stitch through the raised part carefully, as shown.

Or you may pass the stitch through the top of the preceding row. This will depend on the core used; a bunched grass core will be easier to pass through than a solid branch.

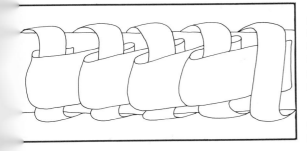

A series of baskets with raffia over reed by Wolfram Krank. He uses only these simple materials so he can concentrate on evolving unusual forms and color. *Courtesy: artist*

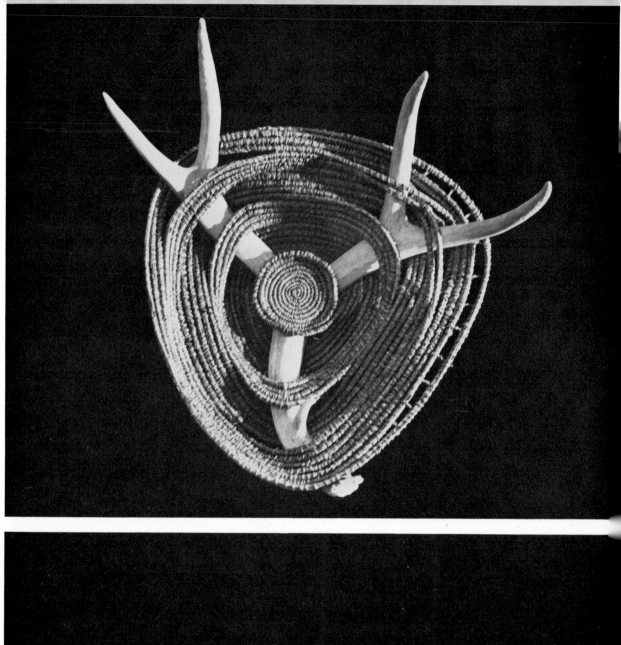

Left:
A deer antler becomes the basis and focal element of a wall sculpture using New Zealand flax coiled over pine needles. 13-inch diameter. By Grace Raymond.

Below left:
LADDER BASKET. Coiling with branches. 6 inches high, 14 inches wide, 14 inches deep. By Carol Shaw-Sutton.

DRY RIVER BASKET. Wrapped linen over grass with branches. Raffia colored details. 13-inch diameter for the back portion, 8 inches for the frontal basket shape. By Carol Shaw-Sutton.

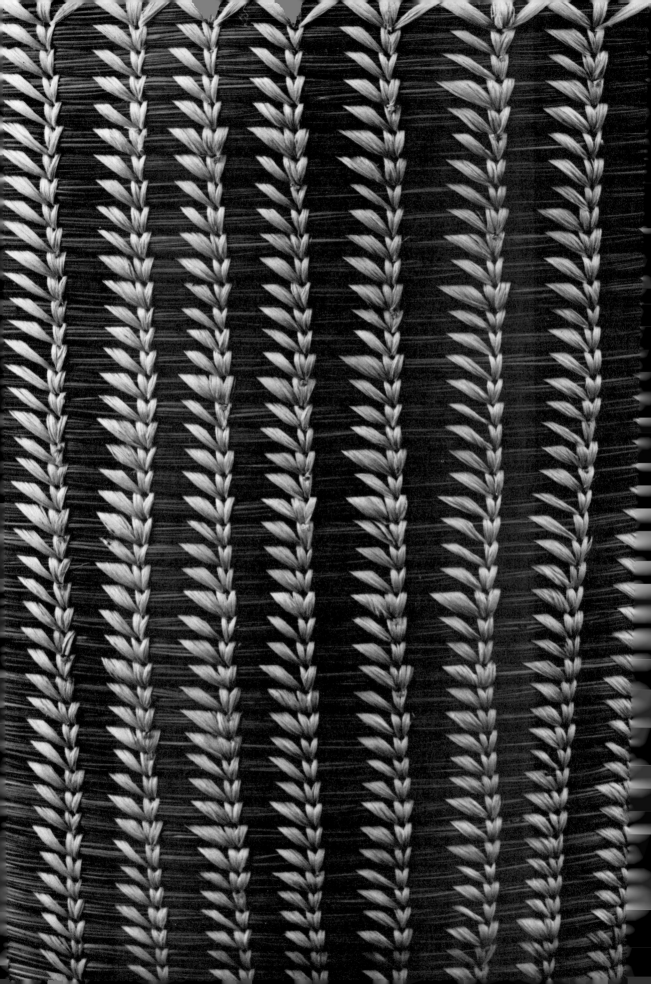

7 PINE-NEEDLE BASKETS

People often become poetic about pine-needle baskets . . . whether they enjoy making them or owning them. The scent of the trees, gathering the pine needles, handling them and feeling the basket evolve by the manipulation of your fingers elicits a response, an inherent sensory experience not attributed to other materials.

Pine-needle baskets are made by coiling a core composed of bunches of needles. The bunches are held together by the wrapping element that may be raffia, thread or fine grass strands. Much of the pine-needle core is exposed and often the needles and the sheaths protrude as compared to close wrapping associated with coiling other materials described in chapter 6.

Making a pine-needle basket is a labor of love that takes patience and time. Needle clusters must be placed "just so" within the core so a unified entity results. The stitches must be studiously placed to form a pattern on the basket and the total shape should be carefully planned and developed.

Pine needles have different characteristics depending on the tree from which they come and the season they are gathered. The length of the needle, which is actually the leaf, may vary from a couple of inches to about 16 inches. The needles seldom grow singly; they usually grow in groups of two to five called "clusters." Each cluster is held together at the end by a scaly covering called the "sheath." In soft pine trees, this sheath falls off as soon as the leaves develop. In the hard-

A coiled pine needle and raffia basket worked in the Double Split Stitch. Coushatta Indians, 1976. 14 inches high. By Marion John. *Courtesy: U.S. Department of the Interior Indian Arts and Crafts Board*

wood pines the sheath does not fall off until the leaves are shed.

To the basketmaker, the length and number of the needles and the sheath characteristics are of prime importance. Long flexible needles are easier to work with than the short, stiff needles. For some baskets, the sheaths are cut off, for others, and for detailing, the sheaths may be left on. Examples of both uses are illustrated.

Gathering pine needles is easy. Nothing could be less expensive. Wherever there is a pine tree the leaves that fall to the ground are picked up and they are ready for use. The needles may be gathered during any season, but the best time is late spring or summer after they have reached full growth and before insect eggs have been deposited on them. Fallen needle clusters are usually beige, reddish brown earth tones. Those that are not fully dried may be placed in the house or away from sun or in a dry, shady place out of doors, for a few weeks.

Needle clusters, or branches with needles, may be picked green (do not damage or defoliate the tree) if you wish to retain some of the green color in your baskets. They must be dried in a shady airy place. Tie them in bunches, lay them on a perforated surface such as screening or hang them, so the air circulates all around them. Turn the needles occasionally during the drying period, but do not let them become moldy. Work with the needles only after they have dried and shrunk. A basket made with fresh pine needles will shrink as it dries, and loosen.

Pine needles may be dyed with natural or synthetic dyes in either the green or dried state. Dyeing them will require some experimentation until you achieve the effect you want. If you dye them with the sheath on, the ends beneath the sheath will remain the original color. When the sheath is removed and allowed to show, the needle tips will make an interesting contrast. If you want the entire needle the dyed color, remove the sheath before dyeing. Dry all needles thoroughly after dyeing.

Assorted types and lengths of pine needles, some dried, some green. Pine cones may also be used for basket decoration.

Pine needle basketry stitches are carried through the top part of the bundle in the coil beneath. The type of stitch used determines the decorative pattern. Most important: For a beautiful, repeat design it is essential to be consistent each time you place the needle through the bundles and next to the previous stitch. Each stitch builds on the previous one, so learn them in the order given.

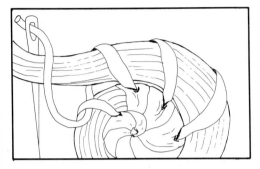

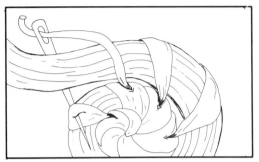

PLAIN STITCH. The same procedure for coiling is used as in basic coiling, page 118. When wrapping pass the sewing needle around the coil and *through* the bundle of pine needles in the preceding coil. Always be consistent as to where you insert the needle through the bundle.

SPLIT STITCH. Pass the needle through the center of the stitch on the preceding coil to split it and also through the top of the pine-needle bundle.

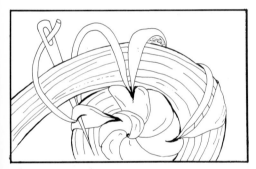

DOUBLE SPLIT STITCH. Each stitch is passed through the stitch on the preceding row *two times* and through the top of the bundle. Bring the second stitch slightly to the left side of the first stitch. Work the Double Split Stitch counterclockwise as you coil.

WING STITCH. The Wing Stitch is a continuation of the Double Split Stitch. Make one complete row of Double Split Stitches *counterclockwise*. Then go back on the same row and, in a *clockwise* direction, add another wing to the right side of the stitch. Insert your needle only once through the top of the Split Stitch. When you reach the beginning of the first Wing Stitch, make a second row of Double Split Stitches counterclockwise, then again make the right half of the wing by reversing in the clockwise direction.

A contemporary lidded coiled pine-needle basket with raffia using the Double Split Stitch. About 7 inches high, 6 inches diameter. By Irene Pfeiffer.

PREPARATION

Materials for pine-needle basketry include raffia for wrapping, pine needles soaking in a jar of water, a terry-cloth towel to soak up excess moisture and to wrap the damp pine needles, clip clothespin as a holding device, blunts and/or sharp-tipped sewing needles, scissors and sharp knives. It is wise to prepare all the pine needles you will probably need before you begin.

When desirable, remove sheath from the pine-needle cluster ends with a sharp knife. . .

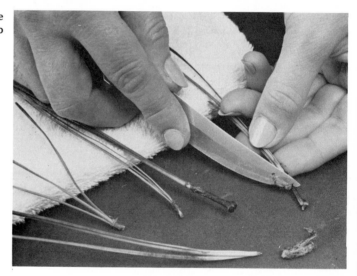

. . . or with your fingernail. It is easier to remove the sheaths from needles that have been soaked. To simplify working, keep the needles in front of you wrapped in a towel, so they are always readily available as you need them.

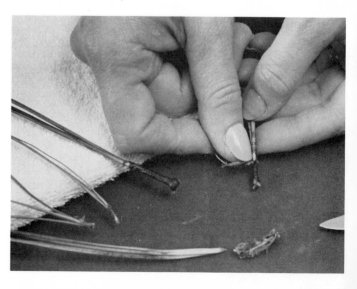

MAKING A BASKET

To begin the coil, it is easier to work with the sheaths in place. Use several clusters of needles (depending on the thickness of the needle and the core desired) and stagger the ends. Begin to wrap with the raffia in the same method shown for coiling, page 117. Try to achieve a rhythmic motion as you wrap, select needles and add them in.

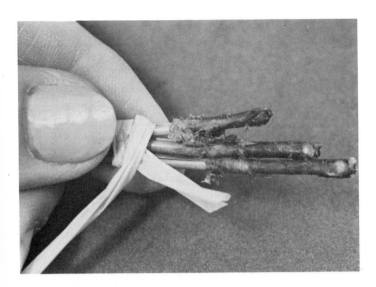

As the coiling evolves, you continuously add in new needles under the core, as shown, to retain the necessary thickness. In this series, the sheaths are on the clusters, but the use of them is optional as you will see in the examples on the following pages. An alternate method for adding needles is shown on the next page.

Closeup detail showing the Plain Stitch on the exposed bunched pine needles. Observe how carefully they have been placed to form a radiating design. A basket can be completed with this stitch only or combined with other pine-needle basketry stitches.

Another method for beginning the basket is illustrated in this series. In the previous demonstration the wrapping was over individual coils and the needles were visible between the stitches (exposed core). In this demonstration, the wrapping completely covers the needles using the same Plain Stitch. Another method for adding pine needles is illustrated: to help keep the core the same thickness as you work. Cut a short length from a plastic straw (about 1½ inches) and place it around the clusters. New needles are continuously inserted through the straw and into the coiling.

A combination of covered and exposed core is used as the basket circumference increases. The visual effect is beautiful. The plastic straw length is constantly moved along the core.

An additional decorative treatment is accomplished by combining the form with a row of needles with the sheaths on them. They protrude purposely, as shown in the photo, below.

The basket bottom combining covered coiling, exposed core and sheathed needles. The basket may be completed using any progression of stitches and combinations of sheathed and unsheathed clusters. *All demonstrations by Dee Menagh*

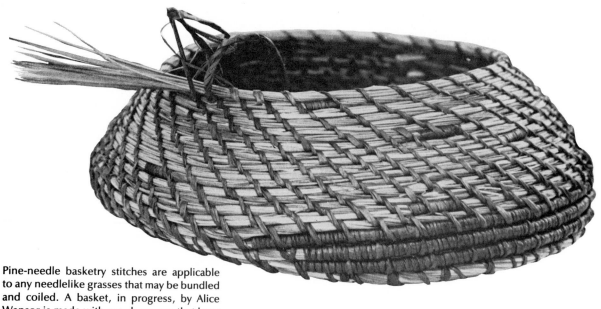

Pine-needle basketry stitches are applicable to any needlelike grasses that may be bundled and coiled. A basket, in progress, by Alice Wansor is made with marsh grasses that have working characteristics very similar to pine needles. Some of the ends have been wrapped so they look like pine needles. 10-inch diameter. *Courtesy: artist*

The Split Stitch worked around coiled pine needles. 4 inches high, 7-inch diameter. By Karen McCarthy. *Courtesy: artist*

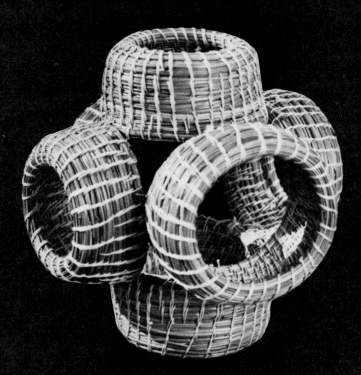

Open-ended pine-needle cylinders are assembled result in a sculptural form. 8 inches high, 8-inch diameter. By Arlan Oftedahl.

Sheathed pine needles protruding along one side of the basket are a textural contrast for the unsheathed ends along the other side. 14 inches high, 9-inch diameter. By Marjorie McBeath.

The oval base for a pine-needle basket is begun by working the initial coils long rather than round. Coiled pine needles are stitched with perl cotton. 7 inches wide. By Dee Menagh.

Patterns can be made over pine-needle coils by changing the directions of the stitches. By Marjorie McBeath. *Courtesy: artist*

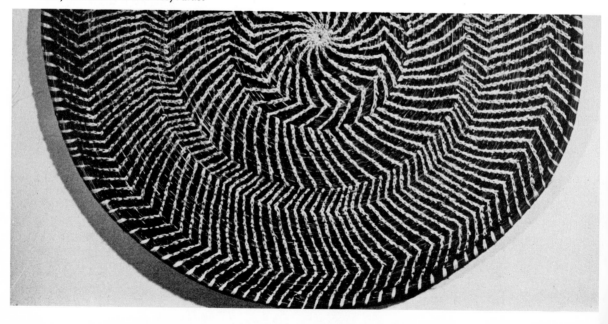

Coiled pine needles stitched with natural and dyed raffia. Closely wrapped raffia is used for the central pattern; The Wing Stitch creates the repeat overall design on the outer coils with the core exposed. Overall basket, 18-inch diameter. By Gerry Henry.

Above:
Unusual embellishments can be added any-where on a coiled pine-needle basket. Sea-shells grouped on one side of the basket interior provide an inventive treatment. Approx. 10-inch diameter. By Susan Marrant.
Photo: Joel Marrant

Below:
Oval pine-needle basket with a Split Stitch worked in a slanted pattern. One row of sheathed needles adds surface detail and variety. 3½ inches high, 6 inches wide. By Frances Meador.

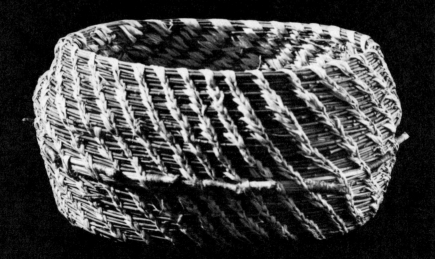

Long pine needles form the core and are allowed to protrude from a coiled basket with fiber wrapping. 8 inches high, 15-inch diameter. By Bonnie Zimmer.

Long thick needles of Jeffrey pine from Washington were used for this basket. Some of the needles flare out from the top rim in opposite directions as a beautiful solution to ending the basket. See bottom detail below. 3½ inches high, 6-inch diameter. By Karen McCarthy.

Pine needles laid in a square were coiled using the sheathed ends on two corners and the
loose ends on the opposite corners. 15 inches
high, 6 inches square. By B. J. Adams. *Photo:
Clark Adams*

Pine needles coiled with raffia in a checkerboard design. Observe how the sizes of the
segments change as the basket base expands
(*below*). 3½ inches high, 5½-inch diameter.
By Karen McCarthy. *Courtesy: artist*

Raffia wrapped over coiled pine needles. The Ziz-Zag Stitch is accomplished using an embroidery concept. An added stitch is placed around two coils to create a different design. (See directions below.) 4 inches high, 6-inch diameter. By Karen McCarthy. *Courtesy: artist*

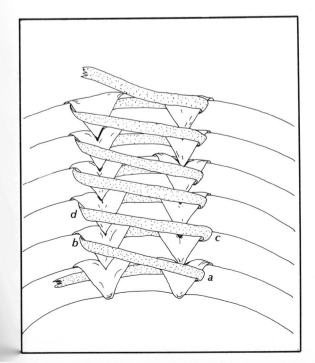

ZIG-ZAG STITCH. An exposed core pine-needle basket has been made with the Split Stitch carefully designed so it is in even radiating rows. The Zig-Zag design is added after the basket is completed. Use the same color or a contrasting color material for the stitch. Bring the needle up at *a*, across and down at *b*, under the stitch only (not inside the basket) and up at *c*, under the stitches again and up at *d* and so forth.

Coiled Torrey pine needles wrapped with raffia worked in the Double Split Stitch. The sheaths were left on the needles for the bottom rows (*below*). The base is solidly coiled and inverted on the inside to emulate an Early American fruit basket. When the fruit is inside, it spreads around the raised interior base so it will not crush. 6 inches long, 6-inch diameter. By Frank Kraynek.

Sheathed Torrey pine needles laid so the sheaths are in vertical rows. The pine needles were dyed; the sheaths absorbed more color than the needles and yield a beautiful tonal range. The basket bottom (*below*) is inverted on the interior to emulate a berry basket. 9 inches high, 9-inch diameter. By Fran Kraynek.

Sheathed pine needles worked with the sheaths close together yield a strong, sturdy exterior surface. 4½ inches high, 7-inch diameter. By Myrna Brunson.

Coiled pine needles stitched with raffia. Elder pine cones are added in along the last coil to form a decorative rim. 4 inches high, 6-inch diameter. By Karen McCarthy. *Courtesy: artist*

Torrey pine needles were dyed brown. The sheaths were left on to form a dye resist. When the sheaths were removed the tips remained light and resulted in a porcupine-quill appearance. 9 inches high, 9-inch diameter. By Fran Kraynek.

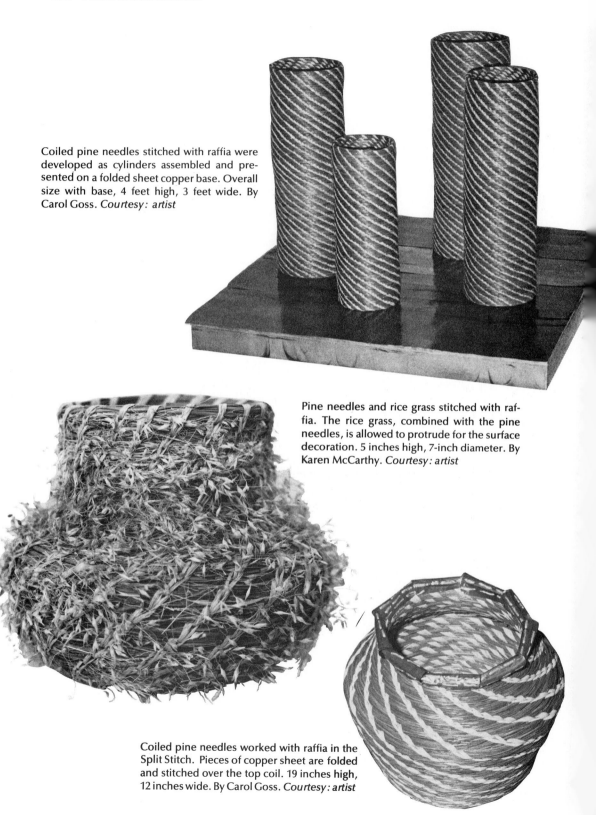

Coiled pine needles stitched with raffia were developed as cylinders assembled and presented on a folded sheet copper base. Overall size with base, 4 feet high, 3 feet wide. By Carol Goss. *Courtesy: artist*

Pine needles and rice grass stitched with raffia. The rice grass, combined with the pine needles, is allowed to protrude for the surface decoration. 5 inches high, 7-inch diameter. By Karen McCarthy. *Courtesy: artist*

Coiled pine needles worked with raffia in the Split Stitch. Pieces of copper sheet are folded and stitched over the top coil. 19 inches high, 12 inches wide. By Carol Goss. *Courtesy: artist*

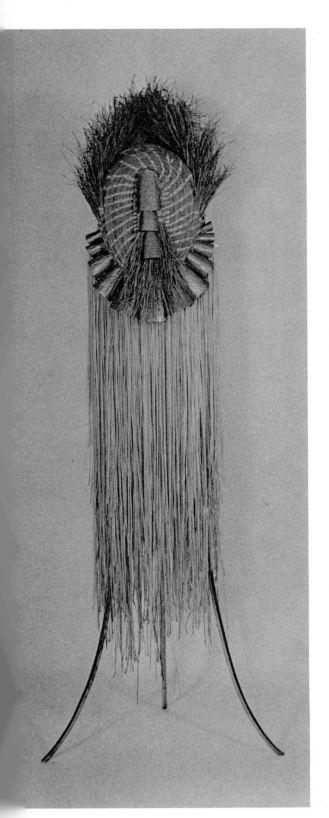

Coiled pine needles wrapped with African palm using the Split Stitch. Shaped copper forms are sewn on. Pine-needle ends protrude at the top and at the center in contrast to the soft cascading strands at the bottom. 60 inches high, 20 inches wide. (See detail, color pages.) By Carol Goss. *Courtesy: artist*

Long pine needles are bunched and tied, then manipulated to form a sculptural roll that is mounted on a box base. 17 inches high, 12 inches wide with base. By Carol Goss. *Courtesy: artist*

8 FREE STYLE

Materials introduced and used in the baskets shown in the preceding chapters were essentially leaves, stems and roots. In this chapter you will discover baskets made from bark and the outer fibrous portions of trees. There are examples of baskets made with previously introduced plant materials but in unusual ways. Also suggested are the application of such nonbasketry techniques as crochet, quilting, knotless netting, and sewing, to basket forms made with a variety of natural materials. They all add up to infinite inspirations designed to jolt your approach to basketry and lead it along new paths.

The American Indian, African, Nordic and other cultures were brilliant in their utilization of birch bark for innumerable objects from small precious containers to large canoes. Examples available in books and museum displays can inspire the use of bark in a variety of forms. Combine the bark with other basketmaking techniques, such as coiling and weaving, so that new forms and new uses for the materials will be born.

When you gather outer tree bark, avoid stripping the material from growing trees so as not to kill or damage the tree. Always select the bark from freshly cut trees that may have been felled in spring or summer when the sap is up. Many trees shed their bark during or after the growing season and materials should be taken at this time. Use some species of palm, eucalyptus and birch. Bark taken from freshly cut trees may be pliable enough to use before it dries out. Older bark may have to be soaked to make it pliable.

Japanese flower basket woven of wide and narrow bamboo strips. 12 inches high, 9 inches wide, 8 inches deep. *Photographed at The Gallery of Oriental Antiques, Palos Verdes Estates, California*

A basketmaking looping technique, used by the Ecuadorians for a soft-sided, colorful basket, is also introduced. The stitch shown may be used with sisal, jute, linen, or with the grasses introduced in earlier chapters. During your own travels, investigate the working methods of peoples from other cultures; it may be a mind-expanding experience. It can possibly make your own creative efforts more personal, more exciting, more individualistic than any amount of research you might glean from a book.

Birch-bark container with incised designs. American Indians of the Great Lakes region. 15 inches high, 12 inches wide. *Photographed at Ideas, Inc., San Diego, California.*

Palm bark and fiber can be manipulated in many inventive ways to make containers. It may be folded, padded and sewn. Usually, it can be found on the ground near a tree after it has been sloughed or blown off.

Palm bark and fiber attached to the tree can be pulled away from the bottom. Pulling off this dead-bottom portion will not hurt the tree. This is a different species than that shown in the photo opposite below.

Eucalyptus bark can be peeled away from a felled log. Do not remove it from a growing tree. Many pieces of bark can be taken from portions of trees that have been cut for logging, land clearance and other reasons.

Manipulated and sewn coconut palm fiber was pulled from the tree and used in its natural state for a free-form container. No soaking or other preparation was necessary. 11 inches high, 10-inch diameter. By Ann Dunn.

Quilted, sewn coconut palm fiber was developed as a lidded box. A cardboard interior armature was used for the box form, which was covered with polyester fill, then with the coconut fiber palm. All were sewn together with cotton twine using the quilting concept. 10 inches high , 10- inch diameter. By Ann Dunn.

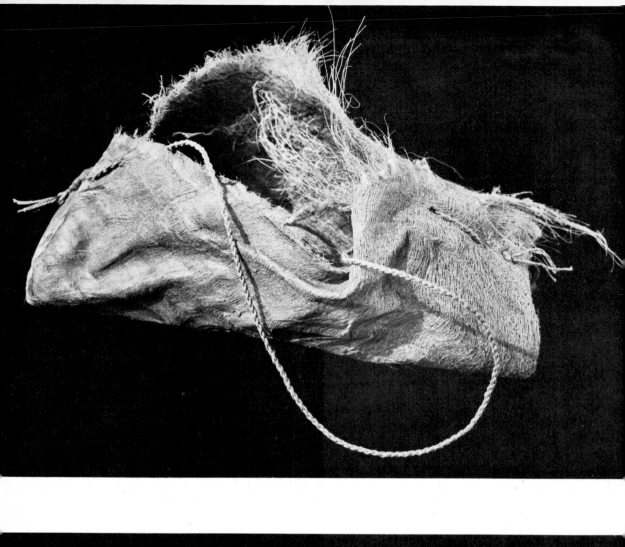
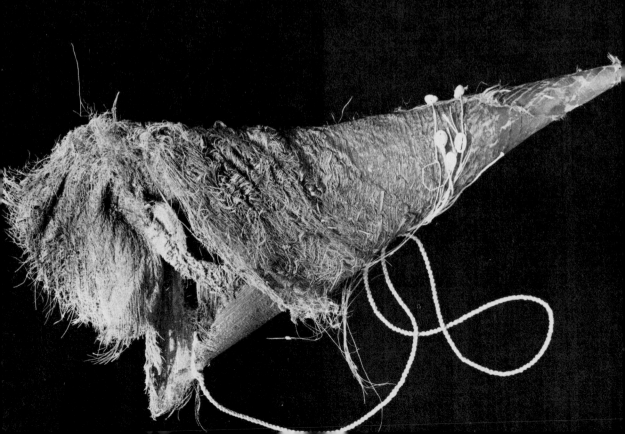

Left:
Above:
Manipulated and sewn date-palm fiber. The sewing elements are raffia and waxed linen. 11 inches long.
Below: The basket was inspired by a quiver used to hold arrows; shells are attached to the string. 24 inches long. By Ann Dunn.

Right:
A flower holder was made from a palm frond sheath. The frond was thoroughly soaked, turned inside out, folded, and the sides sewn together with New Zealand flax. 48 inches high, 30 inches wide, 15 inches deep. By Misti Washington.

A double basket of palm bark manipulated, sewn over an openwork root armature. The hard palm sheath stem end is used for the handle. 23 inches high, 19 inches wide, 10 inches deep. By Frank Kraynek.

A sculptural form in two parts (*see below*) composed of half round and round reed and combined with manipulated palm fibers sewn with cotton thread and raffia. 18 inches high, 18-inch diameter. By Shereen LaPlantz. *Photo: David LaPlantz*

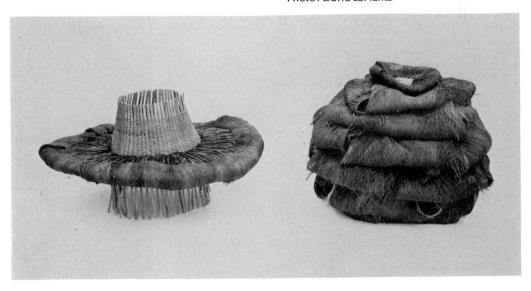

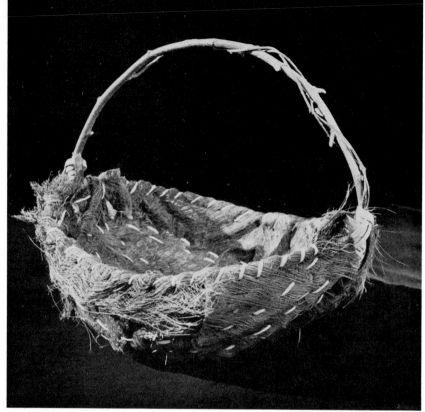

Palm fiber sewn over a twig frame. An elm
branch is used for the handle. 11 inches wide.
By Cindy Schneider.

Detail of the stitching through the palm fiber
and over the twig.

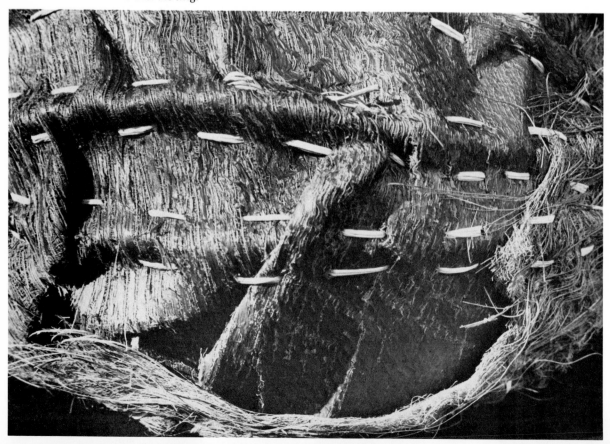

Handmade paper of cattail leaves folded and stitched with gold metallic thread and developed as a container for dried cattails. By Diane Brawarsky. *Photo: Lois Hoberman*

A eucalyptus bark panel, soaked and formed, is placed between the vertical spokes of a twined jute basket. 6 inches high, 13-inch diameter. By Maxine Kirmeyer. *Photo: Carol Craford*

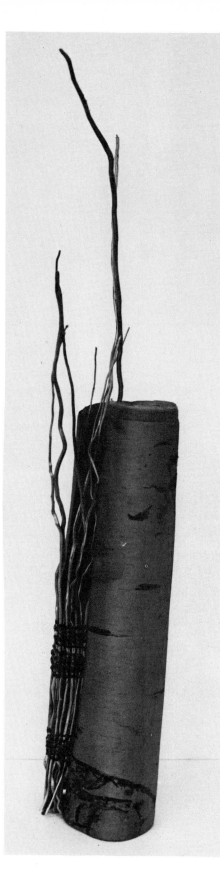

Birch-bark cylinder with spruce roots twined and attached to the bark with raffia. 29 inches high. By Alice Wansor.

A piece of bark in its original cylindrical shape has natural negative areas. It was incorporated as the central decorative and supportive element for a mohair and wool coiled interior form. Approx. 14 inches high, 6-inch diameter. By Betty Ferguson.

Plaited birch-bark strips. The ends were further stripped and shaped to swirl around the basket exterior. 7 inches high. By Alice Wansor.

Soaked and shaped bark was used for the basket sides. Holes were made in the bark with a leather punch. Round reeds were added for spokes and additional reeds were used for the twined sections. 24 inches high, 12-inch diameter. By Susan Marrant. *Photo: Joel Marrant*

MY BAG. Crocheted sea grass with beads and
turkey feathers. The parts were assembled.
Lengths were added into the bottoms of the
bag forms and embellished. 26 inches high, 14
inches wide, 6 inches deep. By Margaret
Henderson. *Photo: John Fecher*

A coiled basket of sea grass. Loose coiling in a
free-form fashion results in an unusual sculptural statement. 36 inches high, 24 inches
wide. By Suellen Glashauser. *Courtesy: artist*

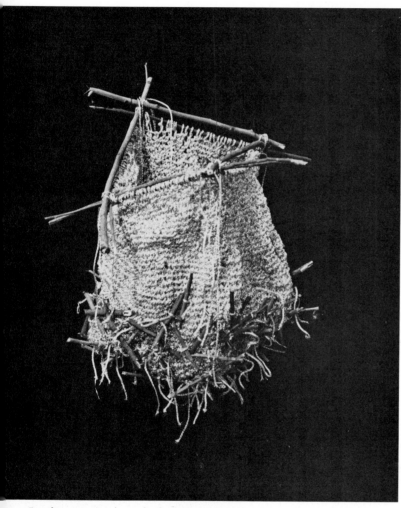

Eucalyptus twigs form the basis for gold metallic thread worked in knotless netting. Additional twigs were inserted around the bottom
circumference. 5 inches high, 4-inch diameter. By Shirley Sestric-Friedlander.

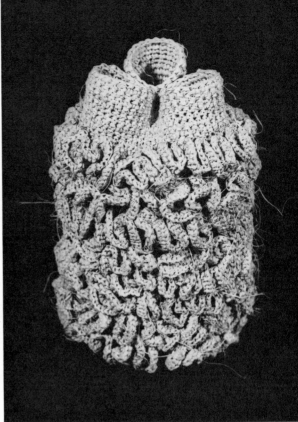

A contemporary statement using crocheted raffia, copper tubing and nylon fishing line. 10 inches high, 6-inch diameter. By John W. Blackman.

Crocheted raffia. 12 inches high, 6-inch diameter. By John W. Blackman. *Photos: Craig Hammell*

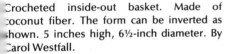

Crocheted inside-out basket. Made of coconut fiber. The form can be inverted as shown. 5 inches high, 6½-inch diameter. By Carol Westfall.

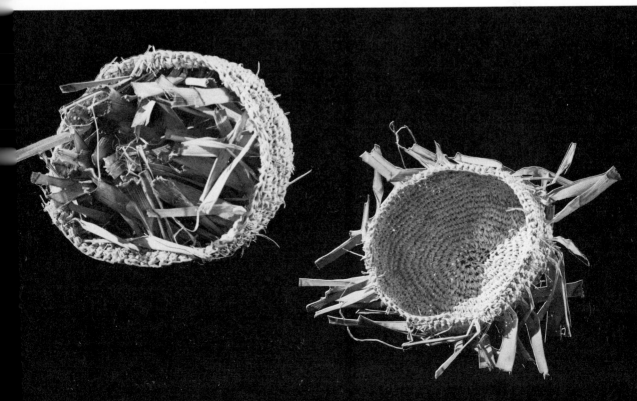

LOOPING

Many cultures use variations of a simple looping technique for baskets. The Ecuadorians make a particularly colorful soft-sided basket with sisal and a tight looping. We offer it here for its application to contemporary baskets with a variety of natural and/or synthetic materials. It is a technique that readily adapts and can be added to other basket forms. The Ecuadorian patterns are surprisingly contemporary. The geometric abstract designs are based on symbolic concepts and motifs taken from South American artifacts. Colors are vivid and marvelously attractive.

You need only a needle and the lengths of fibers with which to work. The natives, both men and women, may be seen walking along the street developing the basket or sitting in the marketplace and stitching them during odd moments.

The stitch is similar to the buttonhole stitch used in surface embroidery. It also resembles a finger-weave technique sometimes referred to as knotless netting and worked in looser looping by the American Indians and in areas of Mexico. The loosely made stitch results in a stretch bag; the tight stitch yields a tight, nonstretchy but very pliable fabric.

1. Make an overhand knot with the thread a over b, as shown, at the end of a long strand or cord threaded in a blunt needle. Leave a small hole in the center so you can bring your needle through it for the first row.

2. Hold on to the knot to prevent it from slipping and bring your needle behind b and up through the hole, over b and through the loop formed by your thread. Pull tightly. Work in a counterclockwise direction.

Continue to stitch around the loop catching the loose end under the stitching as you work until one row is completed. For the second row insert the needle through the top of the first stitch on the preceding row, do not go back through the center again. Continue in this progression until the base diameter is the size you desire.

To shape: As the circumference increases you will have to increase by taking 2 stitches in a stitch of the row below at intervals around the circumference, shown by a and b. Conversely, to decrease, skip stitches in a preceding row to make the circumference narrower.

To change colors: Insert the new color from the back and bring it around and in front of the old color; lay the old color along the work and continue looping with the new color.

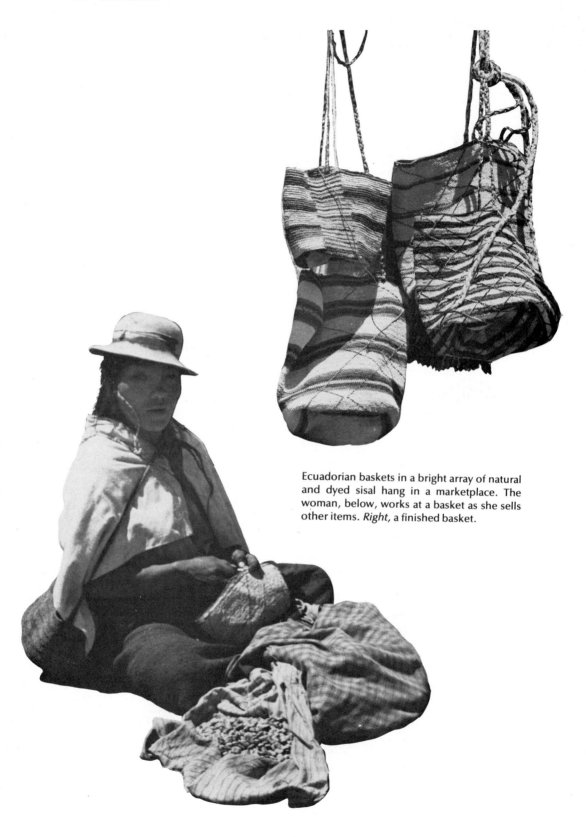

Ecuadorian baskets in a bright array of natural and dyed sisal hang in a marketplace. The woman, below, works at a basket as she sells other items. *Right*, a finished basket.

MASK. Dracaena draco leaves with philodendron sheaths. Plaiting and some wrapping result in an imaginative adaptation of basketry
techniques to sculptural design. The circular
foundation is a branch. The nose is a deer
bone. 32 inches high, 12 inches wide. By Ruth
F. Almstedt.

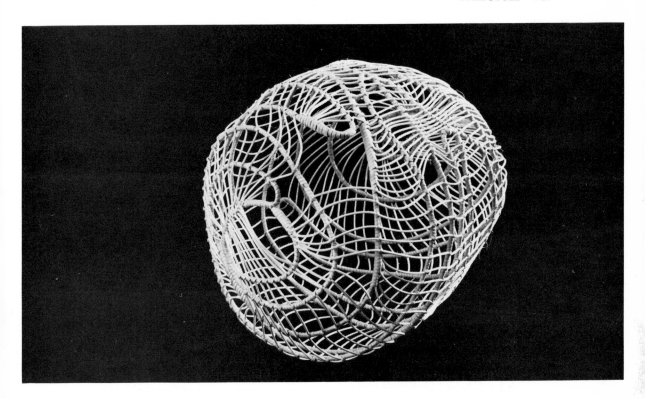

Sculptural forms in a contemporary adaptation of coiling take their inspiration from seashells. *Above,* approx. 18 inches long, 8-inch diameter. By Joan Austin.
Below, 31 inches long and approx. 7-inch diameter at the widest point. By Joan Austin.

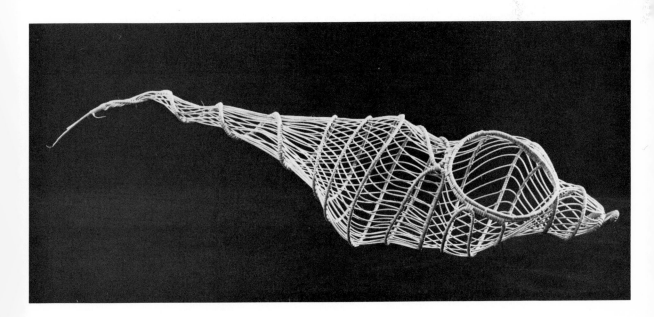

9 QUICK REFERENCE FOR PLANTS AND THEIR USES

The following material has been assembled to serve as a quick reference guide to plants most frequently used in basketmaking. It is a general reference help you become aware of the types of plants and the plant parts used. Traditionally, some of the plants have been used with certain techniques such as weaving or twining. But with the modern approach to basketmaking, all techniques can be applied to many plants and plant parts with imagination and experimentation. Therefore, in the column Techniques Applicable, "all" suggests that the plant and parts are applicable for weaving, twining, plaiting, coiling and free form.

If some of the plants listed are unfamiliar to you, perhaps they do not grow in your locale. Others that are familiar to you may not be listed. If they are usable, use them. The list is not exhaustive but simply a guide to the types of materials you should seek. Consult gardening and botany books and your local nurseryman and park gardeners. Also refer to books listed in the bibliography.

For curing, drying and other preparation processes, refer to chapter 2 and other chapters where specific techniques are illustrated and discussed.

Always experiment with the materials you have available. Study the baskets in the commercial marketplace for the materials used and the techniques. You will find a vast amount of information can be gleaned when you observe baskets closely. It is an exciting, never-ending study that can lead you into scores of exciting discoveries.

A Fiji native plaits a basket with palm.

189

PLANT USE CHART

Plant or General Category	Parts Usable	Miscellaneous Notes	Techniques Applicable
AGAVE	Leaves	Use leaf plain or twisted or Pound leaf on a flat surface and strip out fibers to use for sewing Stripped fibers may also be plied	All
ARTICHOKES	Leaves	Use whole or stripped	All
BRANCHES, FLEXIBLE Cottonwood Red Ozia Elm Sumac Mulberry Weeping Poplar Willow Redbud Willow White Birch and others	Green or dried Use peeled or unpeeled	Boil to remove bark Branches may be used whole or split Colors will vary with seasons picked	All
BARK Birch Fir Cedar Palm Eucalyptus Yew and others	Whole pieces stripped lengths	Be sure all insects are removed	Free style and in combination with other techniques: weaving, twining, plaiting
CATALPA	Pods—dried after they fall from tree	Use whole for decoration or strip into lengths after soaking in warm water 1 hour	Twining Plaiting Stitching for Coiling
CORNHUSKS	Whole husk or stripped into lengths	Gather at harvesttime or buy fresh corn and remove husks Also available predried and packaged in craft shops and ethnic grocery stores	All
DEVIL'S CLAW	Dried pods that look like hooks or claws	Strip into threads	Wrapping material for coiling
FERNS Boston Maidenhair Giant chain almost any variety	Stems	Strip off leaves	All
FLAX New Zealand	Leaves Fresh or dry	Whole or stripped	All
GRASSES, Garden Types	Blades	Gather from gardens and prairies	All
GRASSES, LONG Beach grass Reeds Broom sedge Rye Bunch grass Sweet grass Cattails Wheat Rattlesnake Wire grass Tule	Long Stems Leaves Seed heads	Gather from beaches, cultivated areas, swamps	All

Plant or General Category	Parts Usable	Miscellaneous Notes	Techniques Applicable
LILIES Day Lilies Firecracker Tiger	Leaves Use whole Very effective when twisted	Pick only dried after plant is dormant so as not to injure bulb	All
PALM Most varieties	Fronds Fruit stems Fiber bark	Green or dried in season	All
PINE Most varieties	Needles	Anytime—best in late spring or summer	Mainly coiling, but with other techniques as decorative adjunct
PURCHASED MATERIALS Cane Reed Jute Sea grass Paper fiber Sisal Raffia and others Rattan	All available from craft and weaving suppliers in small and large quantities. Predried, ready for use.		All
ROOTS Alder Sassafras Cattail Sugar Pine Cedar Weeds Ficus Willow Mulberry Yucca Osage and others	Whole or split	With covering or stripped	All
SPLINTS Ash Maple Hickory Oak	From logs See Demonstrations (chapters 2–3)	Take from felled trees	Weaving Plaiting Twining
SPIDER PLANT Different varieties	Leaves	Houseplants	All
TWIGS (See **BRANCHES FLEXIBLE**)			
VINES Boston Ivy Ivy Clematis Virginia English Ivy Creeper Grapevines Wisteria Honeysuckle	Long runners	Household and/or outdoor plant Trim leaves from long runners	All

YUCCA
Dracaena
Dracaena Draco
Filamentosa (Adam's
  Needle)
Whipplei (Our Lord's
  Candle)
	Leaves,
	dried or green
		Whole or split
		New shoots gathered
		in spring are easiest
		to work. But they may
		be gathered year round
		and used
			All

SUBSTANCES TO USE FOR DYEING PLANT MATERIALS

Please note that no guaranteed results are suggested. The dyeing ability of any plant will vary at different times of the year. Weather conditions such as dryness and humidity will also affect the amount of dye color that may be extracted. The following are, of necessity, very loose generalizations based on our own trial and error, and research.

You may discover plants growing in your region that work as well or better than those proposed here. The plant to be dyed and its affinity for the dye color will affect the final appearance.

Generally a mordant is used with manyof the dyes. A mordant is any substance that will combine with a dye substance to form a permanent color. However, this is not always true with materials dyed with vegetable dyes; we all know even the finest materials under optimum, well-controlled conditions can fade from sun and light. Mordants help to make the color fast; without them the color could wash out or fade very quickly.

Mordants are metallic salts such as alum, chrome, copperas and tin available from your drugstore. Vinegar and household salt are also used for mordants in some dyes. Different mordants, mixed in with the dye-bath, may result in different colors for the same dye extract. Tin tends to make colors bright; copperas darkens them and can yield green, purple and purple-black tones; chrome results in shades of golds, brasses and rusts. Sometimes mixing mordants can produce other color combinations. Different amounts of a mordant will also alter the color depth . . . though too much mordant can injure the material being dyed.

Begin a dye solution with a controlled amount of mordant to water ratio such as ½ cup mordant to 1 gallon of water and keep records of the results. Then change the formula as you experiment for different results.

The dyebath is the water that has been colored by the extraction of the plant, berry, twig, root, or bark materials after they have been boiled and strained. The mordant should be placed in the dyebath solution and mixed. Sometimes about ½ cup tartaric acid and Glauber's salts (also chemicals that help set dye color) may be added to the solution halfway through the dye procedure. The plants to be dyed should be carefully placed in the simmering water and watched closely to determine how much dye they absorb and the color depth. They must be handled gently as some can be extremely fragile.

Remove the dyed plant materials from the dyebath carefully and allow to dry thoroughly. Redampen before using them in the baskets. Some of the color may bleed out. Also refer to chapter 2 for additional material about dyes and colorants.

Substance	Part to Use for Dye	Time to Collect	To Preserve Dye Substance	Appropriate Mordant	Color Range
Acorns	Whole or cracked nut	In fall	Use fresh or dry Store dry	Alum	Tans
Beets	Part below ground	Mature and ripe	Fresh	Alum	Tans
Blackberries	Fruit	Ripe	Fresh or frozen	Alum Tin	Browns Purples
Blackberry Vines	1- to 2-year-old vines	Late summer	Fresh	Alum	Red-tans
Black Walnut	Hulls, entire nut, leaves, twigs and bark	Late summer and fall Spring	Use fresh or dry Store dry	Alum Copperas	Browns & tans Blacks & greys
Chrysanthemum blossoms	Blossoms	Full bloom	Fresh or dry Store dry	Alum	Yellows
Coffee	Beans, grounds, powder	Buy from grocer	Usual home storage	Alum	Tans
Concord grapes	Fruit	Ripe	Use fresh	Alum Tin	Lavender, purple Purple
Elderberries	Fruit	Ripe	Fresh or frozen	Alum Chrome Tin	Purples Blues Blue-greens
Hickory bark	Hull from nuts Leaves Twigs, bark	Early fall and late summer Spring	Fresh or dry Store dry	Alum	Rust, tans Rosy beige Some Yellow
Onions Red Yellow	Dry skin Dry skin	Mature bulbs Mature bulbs	Use dry Store dry	Chrome Tin Alum	Gold-tan Red-tan-brown Yellow
Peach	Leaves	Summer and early fall	Fresh	Alum Tin	Yellow Bright yellow
Pokeberries	Berries with some roots and stems	Just before fully ripe	Fresh or frozen	Acid vinegar or salt Tin	Deep purple Bright reds, corals
Roses Floribunda	Canes Leaves	Midsummer to frost	Fresh	Alum Copperas	Tan Dark green and black
Tea	Leaves, Tea bags, Powdered tea	Purchase	Home storage	Alum	Ecru-tans
Turmeric	Powder made from plant	Purchase from grocer	Home storage in dry place	Alum Chrome	Yellow Gold and brass
Wild Grapes	Fruit	Ripe	Fresh or frozen	Alum	Lavenders

SUPPLY INFORMATION

Suppliers of prepared basketry materials can be readily found by consulting the yellow pages of your local telephone book under craft suppliers, art supplies, handicrafts, weavers' supplies or other similar listing depending on your locale. Also seek ads for these materials in such craft publications as *Creative Crafts, Fiberarts, Shuttle Spindle & Dyepot, Craft Horizons, McCall's Needlework, The Goodfellow Review of Crafts,* and such art education magazines as *The Instructor Magazine* and *Arts and Activities,* scouting publications and so forth. For a state by state listing of suppliers of applicable materials consult the *Contemporary Crafts Marketplace* (annual editions) usually available at your library. In these publications you will be able to locate shops near you and mail order suppliers for sea grass, cane, reed, rattan, jute, sisal and other prepared materials.

Since the thrust of this book is to gather your own materials and prepare them for basketry, your most readily available sources for materials are your own houseplants and gardens, local prairies, swamps, seashores, canyons, desert areas, forest preserves, garden and nursery supply companies and the great outdoors wherever plants grow. Please adhere to local plant protection laws (see chapter 2) for the sake of the environment as well as for your own law-abiding conscience.

SELECTED
BIBLIOGRAPHY

Allen, Elsie. *Pomo Basketmaking*. Healdsburg, California: Naturegraph Publishers, 1972.

Austin, Robert, and Ueda, Koichiro. *Bamboo*. New York and Tokyo: A Weatherhill Book, 1970.

Bobart, H. H. *Basketwork Through the Ages*. London, England: Oxford University Press, 1936.

Brigham, William Tufts. *Mat and Basket Weaving of the Ancient Hawaiians*. Honolulu, Hawaii: Bishop Museum Press, 1906.

Christopher, F. V. *Basketry*. New York: Dover Publications, 1952.

Consumer Guide, ed. *Basketry* (Twining). Skokie, Ill.: Publications Int., Ltd., 1978.

Cooke, Viva J., and Sampley, Julia M. *Palmetto Braiding and Weaving*. Miami, Florida: E. A. Seemann Publishing, Inc., 1947.

Dendel, Esther Warner. *The Basic Book of Twining*. New York: Van Nostrand Reinhold, 1978.

Emery, Irene. *The Primary Structures of Fabrics*. Washington, D.C.: The Textile Museum, 1966.

Fitzgerald, Sallie G. *Lessons in Reed Weaving*. Boston: The Priscilla Publishing Co., 1924.

Gilman, Rachel Seidel, and Bess, Nancy. *Step by Step Basketry*. New York: Golden Press, 1977.

Glashauser, Suellen, and Westfall, Carol. *Plaiting, Step-by-Step*. New York: Watson-Guptill Publications, 1976.

Hart, Dan and Carol. *Natural Basketry*. New York: Watson-Guptill Publications, 1976.

James, George Wharton. *Indian Basketry*. New York: Dover Publications, 1972. Reprint of 1909 Edition.

————. *Poetry and Symbolism of Indian Basketry*. Point Loma, California: George Wharton James, 1913.

Lesch, Alma. *Vegetable Dyeing*. New York: Watson-Guptill Publications, 1970.

Linsley, Leslie. *Wildcrafts*. Garden City, New York: Doubleday & Co., Inc., 1977.

Mason, Otis Tufton. *Aboriginal American Basketry*. Glorieta, New Mexico: The Rio Grande Press, Inc., 1972. Reprint of 1902 edition.

Meilach, Dona Z. *A Modern Approach to Basketry with Fibers and Grasses*. New York: Crown Publishers, Inc., 1974.

Navajo School of Indian Basketry. *Indian Basket Weaving*. New York: Dover Publications. 1971.

Newman, Sandra Corrie. *Indian Basket Weaving*. Flagstaff, Arizona: Northland Press, 1974.

Rossbach, Ed. *Baskets as Textile Art*. New York: Van Nostrand Reinhold Company, 1973.

————. *The New Basketry*. New York: Van Nostrand Reinhold Company, 1976.

Schetky, Ethel Jane, and staff, eds. *Dye Plants and Dyeing—A Handbook*. Brooklyn, New York: Brooklyn Botanic Garden, 1964.

Stephens, Cleo M. *Willow Spokes and Wickerwork*. Harrisburg, Pennsylvania: Stackpole Books, 1975.

Stephenson, Sue H. *Basketry of the Appalachian Mountains*. New York: Van Nostrand Reinhold Company, 1977.

Teleki, Gloria Roth. *The Baskets of Rural America*. New York: E. P. Dutton & Co., Inc., 1975.

Thresh, Robert and Christine. *An Introduction to Natural Dyeing*. Santa Rosa, California: Thresh Publications, 1972.

Tod, Osma Gallinger. *Earth Basketry*. New York: Crown Publishers, Inc., Bonanza Books, 1968.

Whiteford, Andrew Hunter. *North American Indian Arts*. New York: Golden Press, 1970.

Wilkins, Marilyn, *California Dye Plants*. Santa Rosa, California: Thresh Publications, 1976.

PAMPHLETS

Denver Art Museum, Department of Art, Denver, Colorado
Leaflet No. 5   Pima Indian Close Coiled Basketry. 1930.

Leaflet No. 17   Hopi Indian Basketry. 1931.

Leaflet No. 67   Basketry Construction Technics. 1935.

Leaflet No. 68   Basketry Decoration Technics. 1935.

Leaflets 83–84   The Main Divisions of California Indian Basketry. 1937.

Leaflet No. 88   Types of Southwestern Coiled Basketry. 1951.

Leaflets 99–100   Southwestern Twined, Wicker, and Plaited Basketry. 1940.

BOTANY AND ENCYCLOPEDIAS

Americana
Encyclopaedia Britannica
The World Book
Listings under: Botany
                 Plants
                 Shrubs
                 Trees
                 Vines

GARDENING BOOKS

Better Homes and Gardens Garden Book. Des Moines, Iowa: Meredith Publishing Co., 1951.

Clark, David E., ed. *SUNSET Western Garden Book.* Menlo Park, California: Sunset Publishing Co., 1967. Rev. 1973.

INDEX